FACT FILE 2015
Statistics brought alive

All the facts and statistics you need to understand our world.
In print in this book & online as part of
Complete Issues

Complete Issues
articles · statistics · contacts

Complete Issues
articles · statistics · contacts
www.completeissues.co.uk

Your log in details:

Username: _____

Password: _____

Fact File 2015

The statistics behind the issues and controversies

Fact File 2015 is part of Complete Issues, a unique combination of resources online and in print.

Complete Issues

Complete Issues gives you the statistics, articles and contacts to understand the world we live in.

The unique format means that this information is available on the shelf and on the screen.

How does Complete Issues work?

Using **www.completeissues.co.uk** you can view individual pages from this book on screen, download, print, use on whiteboards and adapt to suit your needs. We provide you with the raw data we used to make the charts. This makes Fact File even more flexible and useful.

As well as being able to access all these statistics in PDF format, there are references and links to other parts of Complete Issues and to the sources we used.

The statistics in Fact File, the articles in the Essential Articles series and online contacts work beautifully together on the Complete Issues website to produce a choice of relevant data, opinion and links.

When you search for a topic you instantly generate a list of relevant articles, figures and organisations with a thumbnail of the page and a short description.

The advantages of Complete Issues over just googling are:

- varied & reliable sources
- moderated - so appropriate for student use
- properly referenced
- beautifully presented
- adaptable for classroom use
- cleared for copyright
- links that are checked for safety and relevance

Users can search and browse individual elements of Complete Issues or all the parts together, past and present editions.

Students can search for statistics secure in the knowledge that they will find meaningful data from reliable sources.

In addition to the online service, you have this attractive printed version always available. Its clear presentation encourages users to feel confident about using and understanding statistical information and to browse and enjoy the data.

Because you have both the book and online access you can use Fact File in different ways with different groups and in different locations. It can be used simultaneously in the library, in the classroom and at home.

Your purchase of the book gives you access to Fact File PDFs on one computer at a time. You can find your access codes on your covering letter or by contacting us. It is useful to record them on page 1 of this volume.

You can also buy an online expansion pack with an unlimited site licence to make the service and the material available to all students and staff at all times, even from home. This also unlocks additional features such as interactive graphs and the search facility.

If you do not yet have the other resources in Complete Issues - the articles and the contacts - you can sample the service and upgrade here:

www.completeissues.co.uk

Complete Issues
articles · statistics · contacts

Published by Carel Press Ltd
4 Hewson St, Carlisle CA2 5AU

Tel +44 (0)1228 538928, Fax 591816

office@carelpress.co.uk

www.carelpress.com
© Carel Press

Research, design and editorial team:
Anne Louise Kershaw, Debbie Maxwell, Christine A Shepherd, Chas White

Cover design: Anne Louise Kershaw

Subscriptions: Ann Batey (Manager),
Brenda Hughes, Anne Maclagan

British Library Cataloguing in Publication Data
A catalogue record for this book is available from the British Library

ISBN 978-1-905600-47-2

Printed by Finemark, Poland

FACT FILE 2015 CONTENTS

ANIMALS

8 Animal research
Most people accept the need to use animals for medical research but they are less likely to support animal testing for other purposes.

11 Stray dogs
29% of UK owners will lose their dog at least once during the pet's lifetime. What happens to these strays?

14 Pet population
Almost half of UK households contain a pet. That's around 65 million animals.

ART & CULTURE

16 Culture fix
Are we taking part in fewer cultural activities... or just changing how we are experiencing them?

18 Graffiti
Is it creative or just destructive? Street art or vandalism? Opinions on graffiti are divided.

20 Visitor attractions
Cultural venues such as museums and art galleries feature strongly among the places most people like to visit.

22 Reading habits
72% of people enjoy reading - but 6% think it is pointless!

24 Museums at night
This annual event allows people to visit a museum after normal opening hours - and people love it!

BODY IMAGE

26 Body issues
Pressures on young girls mean that 90% of them try to change their appearance in some way.

28 Looking good
Both men and women worry about their looks - but their concerns are not the same.

30 Cosmetic surgery
There were more than 50,000 cosmetic surgery operations carried out in Britain in 2013. 90% of these were on women.

32 Body art
Views on tattoos from those who have them and those who don't.

BRITAIN AND ITS CITIZENS

36 As others see us
What people from other countries think about the UK and its inhabitants.

39 Role models
Do famous people have a duty to use their influence in a good cause? And should they always behave properly because they set an example to others?

42 Political participation
We may be losing interest in politics but people have found other ways to show their concerns about issues.

44 Small talk
Most people find that a chat with their neighbours makes them feel happier.

46 Giving thanks
Saying thank you is important and on average we do it 32 times a day.

48 Phobias
Our greatest fears.

"Just cause I'm heavily tattooed doesn't mean I'm nasty, scary or stupid."

page 34

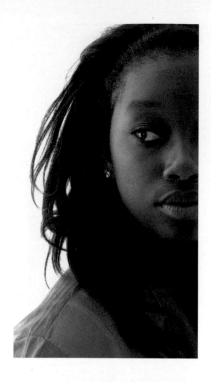

"Bullying is something that will haunt me for the rest of my life"

page 56

BULLYING

50   Bullying: The myths and the facts
Whatever form it takes, bullying is not just a normal part of growing up.

52   Reporting bullying
More than 44,000 youngsters who contacted ChildLine had concerns about bullying.

54   Impact of bullying
Almost half of 13-18 year olds said they had experienced bullying and for some the damaging effects were long lasting.

58   Cyberbullying
Millions of young people have experienced cyberbullying and for some it has been a daily experience.

EDUCATION

62   Disruptive behaviour
How much does bad behaviour in class actually affect learning time?

64   School costs
Even though state education is free, parents need to find money for 'extras' - which are actually essentials. Young people collected this information about how the poorest amongst them miss out.

66   Education & technology
Almost half of pupils take at least one gadget to school - and a majority rely on technology for doing homework.

68   Religious schools
A significant proportion of UK schools are associated with particular religions. How many schools and how many pupils?

70   World class education
Our universities are among the best in the world and are one of the most attractive things about the country.

ENVIRONMENT

72   Climate or coal?
For electricity production coal is cheaper to use than gas - but the consequences for the environment are serious.

74   Climate change & travel
Most people believe that car and plane use causes climate change, but will they change their behaviour?

76   Climate change & attitudes
Protecting the environment is an important issue for many people - and they think more could be done.

FAMILY & RELATIONSHIPS

80   Family & career
Girls today are ambitious, but worry about balancing work and family life in the future.

82   Living with parents
More young adults are living with their parents - but why are more men than women staying in their childhood home?

84   Sex, marriage & parenthood
Attitudes to sex before marriage have become more relaxed, but marriage is seen as important if you want to have children.

86   Separation & divorce
35,000 young people contacted ChildLine last year with worries about family problems.

FINANCE

89   Students & money
Students have deep concerns about their finances and still have to rely on support from their parents - especially in emergencies.

92   Social life
We overspend when we are out with friends because we don't want to look mean - so we end up in 'social debt'.

94 Family spending
What do families spend their money on? Average weekly household spending in the UK.

96 Spending power
The way we measure inflation has changed over time. A look back shows us how we used to live.

GENDER

99 Facing the issues
Body image, self-esteem, relationships, everyday sexism – these are just some of the issues girls battle with on a daily basis.

102 Gender & family life
There is less support for a traditional division of roles in the home yet women are still burdened with more domestic chores.

104 Equality
The majority of people believe women should be equal to men, yet many women still don't believe they are treated that way.

HEALTH

107 Neglected health
UK's Mr and Mrs Average are not in average health, but are in fact tired, overweight, dehydrated and unfit!

110 Sickness absence
131 million days were lost to ill health in 2013, that's 4.4 days for every worker.

112 Abortions
The facts about the number, timing and frequency of terminations.

115 Causes of death
Medical advances in the treatment of many illnesses and diseases mean that death rates are generally falling. So what are the greatest health problems?

118 Salt
Consuming too much salt is linked to more than 4,000 preventable deaths per year. We need to be aware of how much we are eating and where it is hidden.

LANGUAGE

122 Accents
People are prepared to judge how friendly, intelligent and trustworthy you are by the way you speak. And that's bad news for the people of Liverpool.

125 Lost in translation
It is lack of time, not lack of interest that stops us Brits learning the language of our holiday destinations.

128 Language barriers
Many British holidaymakers struggle with languages and culture.

LAW & ORDER

131 Violence against women
The world's biggest survey on women's experiences of violence reveals the extent of abuse suffered at home, work, in public and online.

134 Perceptions of the police
Most young people have a positive view of the police - but age, gender and ethnicity can all make a difference.

136 Children & crime
"It's just something that happens" - experiences and views of crime among 10 to 15 year olds.

138 Retail crime
Criminal activity by a small number of people costs millions and affects businesses, employees and honest shoppers.

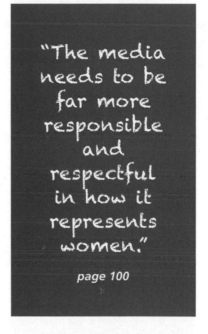

"The media needs to be far more responsible and respectful in how it represents women."

page 100

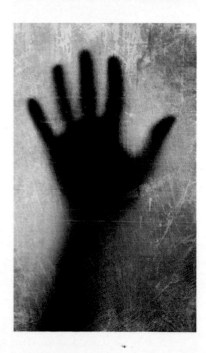

Photo courtesy of Peter Trimming, Flickr

"I am really proud of the fact that I'm helping others, and having a job has given me back my sense of self worth."

page 181

SPORT

142 It's only a game
Is there too much emphasis on competition in children's sport?

144 Inequality in sport
Is sport sexist? There are still huge differences in male and female earnings and in media coverage.

148 Cup fever
A history of the World Cup: winners, goals, games and attendances.

150 Running for charity
Running for charity has become hugely popular – about five millions Britons have done this in the past year.

WAR & CONFLICT

154 Afghanistan: Final toll
British troops ended their combat operation in October 2014 - what was the cost of their involvement?

156 Journalists in danger
Every year journalists and their support workers face serious dangers while doing their jobs.

158 Journalists in exile
Every year, dozens of journalists are forced to leave their home country under threat of imprisonment, torture, violence, or even death.

160 Journalists in prison
Free speech is not guaranteed in every country. Around the world, 124 journalists were jailed on 'anti-state' charges.

162 Cost of peace
United Nations peacekeeping helps countries that are torn by conflict to create conditions for lasting peace.

164 War & peace
Which are the most peaceful countries in the world? And the least?

WIDER WORLD

166 Force of nature
In 2013, 108 countries were hit by natural disasters such as floods, earthquakes and extreme temperatures – the UK was among them.

168 World Giving Index
People were asked if they had given money, time or help in the past month. The best-off countries are not always the most generous with their money.

172 Ebola: The facts
The 2014 epidemic has killed more than all other known Ebola outbreaks combined. Just how dangerous is this disease?

174 Malaria
About 3.4 billion people are at risk of malaria - approximately half of the world's population. Yet it can be prevented and cured.

YOUNG PEOPLE

178 Who do you admire?
The most inspirational figures for young people in the UK.

180 How do you feel?
Unemployment, underachievement at school or growing up in poverty can have a big impact on well-being.

183 What bothers young people?
Youngsters are having to deal with serious issues... and they are facing these concerns at a younger age.

186 Self-harm
Self-harm seems to be increasing as amounts of stress increase: some facts and some suggestions for helping.

189 Looking forward
The views of young people growing up in uncertain times.

192 Index

Animals

Animal research

Attitudes towards the use of animals in scientific research

Overall, the public accepts animal research – but support for medical research is higher than for non-medical research.

How much do you agree or disagree with these statements?

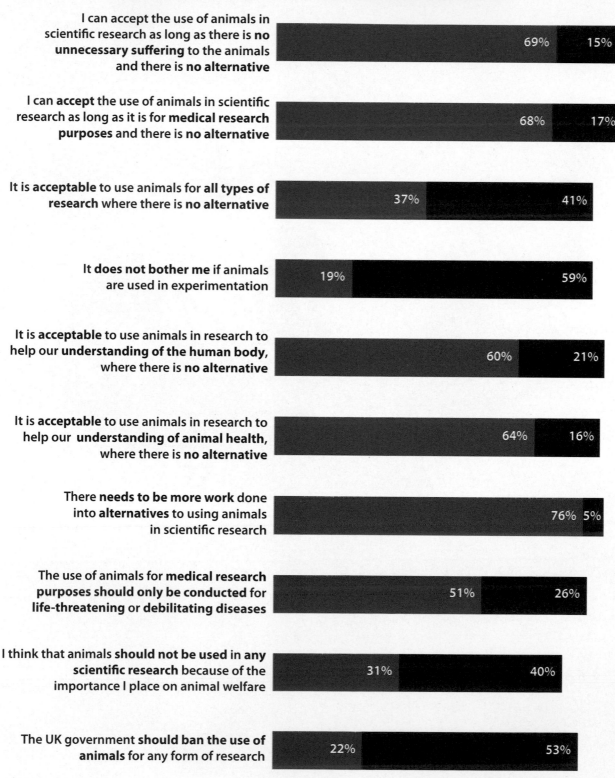

I can accept the use of animals in scientific research as long as there is **no unnecessary suffering** to the animals and there is **no alternative** — 69% / 15%

I can **accept** the use of animals in scientific research as long as it is for **medical research purposes** and there is **no alternative** — 68% / 17%

It is **acceptable** to use animals for **all types of research** where there is **no alternative** — 37% / 41%

It **does not bother me** if animals are used in experimentation — 19% / 59%

It is **acceptable** to use animals in research to help our **understanding of the human body**, where there is **no alternative** — 60% / 21%

It is **acceptable** to use animals in research to help our **understanding of animal health**, where there is **no alternative** — 64% / 16%

There **needs to be more work** done into **alternatives** to using animals in scientific research — 76% / 5%

The use of animals for **medical research purposes should only be conducted** for **life-threatening** or **debilitating diseases** — 51% / 26%

I think that animals **should not be used** in **any scientific research** because of the importance I place on animal welfare — 31% / 40%

The UK government **should ban the use of animals** for any form of research — 22% / 53%

A very small proportion of people said they didn't know and the remaining people neither agreed nor disagreed

The people surveyed were asked to choose which types of animal (if any) they felt were acceptable to use in these different types of research: medical research to benefit people, research into animal health and environmental research.

Rats and mice were chosen as the most acceptable for all, followed by pigs, fish, amphibians and small mammals.

This is largely in line with current practice in the UK.

Species of animal used in procedures* , GB, 2013

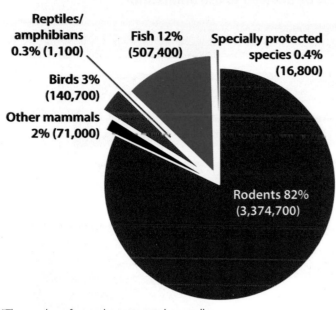

Reptiles/amphibians 0.3% (1,100)

Fish 12% (507,400)

Specially protected species 0.4% (16,800)

Birds 3% (140,700)

Other mammals 2% (71,000)

Rodents 82% (3,374,700)

*The number of procedures reported generally corresponds to the number of animals. A procedure, as regulated by law, is an experiment (or other scientific procedure) that may have the effect of causing an animal pain, suffering, distress or lasting harm

Non-medical animal research

It is acceptable to use animals in scientific research to test...

■ Strongly agree/ tend to agree	■ Neither/nor	■ Strongly disagree/ tend to disagree	■ Don't know

...chemicals that could harm people

| 41% | 19% | 38% | 1% |

...chemicals that could harm pets, farm animals or wildlife

| 38% | 23% | 37% | 2% |

...chemicals that could harm plants or the environment

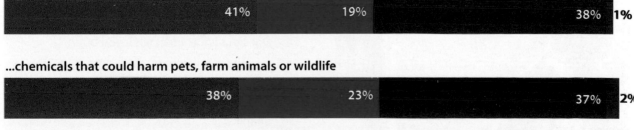

| 23% | 24% | 52% | 1% |

Figures may not add up to 100% due to rounding

Informed

Only **30%** of respondents felt well informed about the use of animals in UK scientific research and **24%** felt they were not at all informed.

The use of animals to test cosmetics products or their ingredients is **banned** in the UK and all other member states of the EU. Since March 2013,

it has also been illegal to sell cosmetics products within the EU which have been newly tested on animals.

31% of respondents thought that animal testing of cosmetics was still allowed with the applicable licence.

Respondents were asked which types of animal research they thought researchers SHOULD be allowed to use animals for

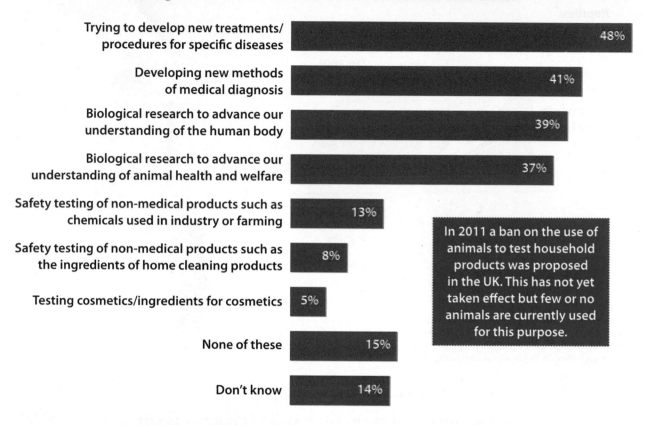

Trying to develop new treatments/ procedures for specific diseases	48%
Developing new methods of medical diagnosis	41%
Biological research to advance our understanding of the human body	39%
Biological research to advance our understanding of animal health and welfare	37%
Safety testing of non-medical products such as chemicals used in industry or farming	13%
Safety testing of non-medical products such as the ingredients of home cleaning products	8%
Testing cosmetics/ingredients for cosmetics	5%
None of these	15%
Don't know	14%

In 2011 a ban on the use of animals to test household products was proposed in the UK. This has not yet taken effect but few or no animals are currently used for this purpose.

Some issues

- Why do people feel differently about the use of different animals in testing?

- Where would you, personally, draw the line on testing on animals?

- Does this issue affect what you buy?

- How do you know if what you buy has been tested on animals?

- What alternatives are there to testing on animals?

NB 969 GB adults aged 15+. (This is a small base therefore care needs to be taken when comparing answers).

Source: Ipsos MORI for the Department for Business, Innovation & Skills
© Crown copyright 2014 www.gov.uk www.ipsos-mori.com
Annual Statistics of Scientific Procedures on Living Animals,
Home Office © Crown copyright 2014 www.gov.uk
RSPCA www.rspca.org.uk

Stray dogs

Despite falling numbers of strays and abandoned dogs, 29% of UK owners will still lose their dog at least once during the pet's lifetime

Dog owners

72% of dog owners didn't know that they only have seven days to collect a missing dog from a local authority before he/she is rehomed or potentially put to sleep

On average, dog owners thought they had 15 days to get their dog back, more than double the time allocated. This may help to account for the estimated **7,805** dogs that were unnecessarily destroyed in 2014.

64% of owners don't know whose responsibility it is to care for missing strays. **46%** said they would get in touch with a family member or neighbour, rather than correctly calling the local council.

Most owners think of their dog as one of the family – **20%** of owners said they had taken time off work because of a missing dog – either to search for him/her or because they were upset at their pet having gone missing.

On average, dog owners were absent from work for **4.2 days** when their dog went missing. **61%** of those dog owners said they'd be too embarrassed to talk about their absence openly with colleagues – choosing instead to explain their time off as 'annual leave' **(63%)**, or 'compassionate leave' **(33%)**.

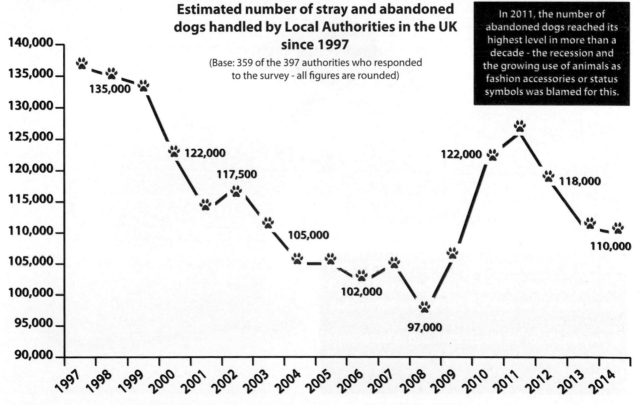

Estimated number of stray and abandoned dogs handled by Local Authorities in the UK since 1997

(Base: 359 of the 397 authorities who responded to the survey - all figures are rounded)

In 2011, the number of abandoned dogs reached its highest level in more than a decade - the recession and the growing use of animals as fashion accessories or status symbols was blamed for this.

135,000
122,000
117,500
105,000
102,000
97,000
122,000
118,000
110,000

What happens to stray dogs?

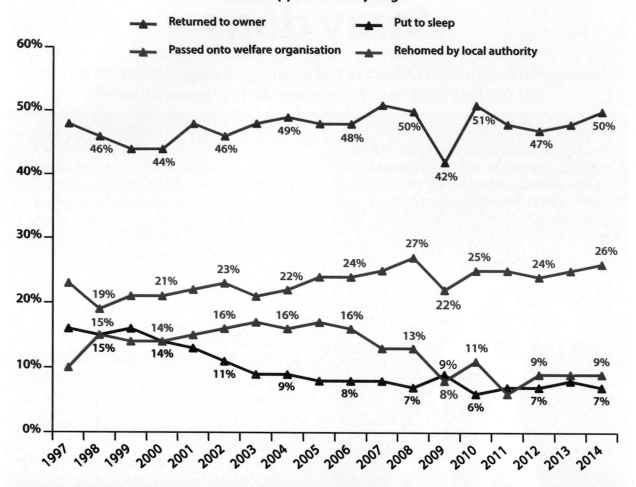

Legend:
- ▲ Returned to owner
- ▲ Put to sleep
- ▲ Passed onto welfare organisation
- ▲ Rehomed by local authority

Rehomed by local authority (top line):
1997: 48%, 1998: 46%, 1999: 44%, 2000: 44%, 2001: 48%, 2002: 46%, 2003: 48%, 2004: 49%, 2005: 48%, 2006: 48%, 2007: 50%, 2008: 50%, 2009: 42%, 2010: 51%, 2011: 47%, 2012: 47%, 2013: 48%, 2014: 50%

Passed onto welfare organisation:
1997: 23%, 1998: 19%, 1999: 21%, 2000: 21%, 2001: 22%, 2002: 23%, 2003: 21%, 2004: 22%, 2005: 24%, 2006: 24%, 2007: 25%, 2008: 27%, 2009: 22%, 2010: 25%, 2011: 25%, 2012: 24%, 2013: 25%, 2014: 26%

Returned to owner:
1997: 10%, 1998: 15%, 1999: 14%, 2000: 14%, 2001: 15%, 2002: 16%, 2003: 17%, 2004: 16%, 2005: 17%, 2006: 16%, 2007: 13%, 2008: 13%, 2009: 9%, 2010: 11%, 2011: 6%, 2012: 9%, 2013: 9%, 2014: 9%

Put to sleep:
1997: 16%, 1998: 15%, 1999: 16%, 2000: 14%, 2001: 13%, 2002: 11%, 2003: 9%, 2004: 9%, 2005: 8%, 2006: 8%, 2007: 8%, 2008: 7%, 2009: 8%, 2010: 6%, 2011: 6%, 2012: 7%, 2013: 7%, 2014: 7%

An estimated 7,805 strays were put to sleep by local authorities in 2013/14 - which amounts to 21 a day

Reasons for destruction were given in **55%** of cases: **2,083** due to behavioural problems or aggression, **1,042** due to ill health, and **755** under the Dangerous Dogs Act.

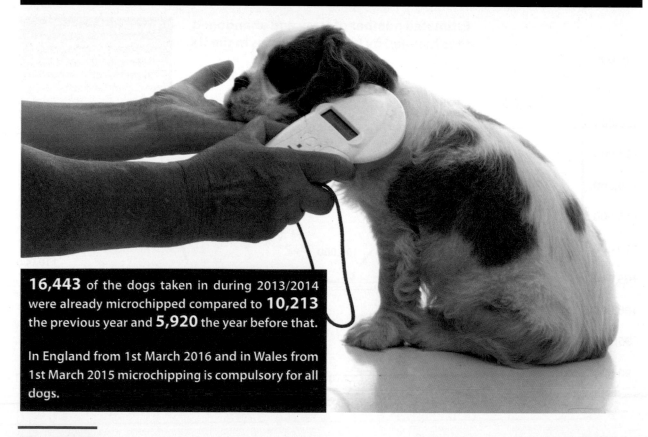

16,443 of the dogs taken in during 2013/2014 were already microchipped compared to **10,213** the previous year and **5,920** the year before that.

In England from 1st March 2016 and in Wales from 1st March 2015 microchipping is compulsory for all dogs.

The method for successfully reuniting strays with their owners was given for **52%** of cases - **25,937** dogs. (More than one method may have been recorded)

Main ways in which dogs were reunited with their owners*

(Base: 333 GB authorities)

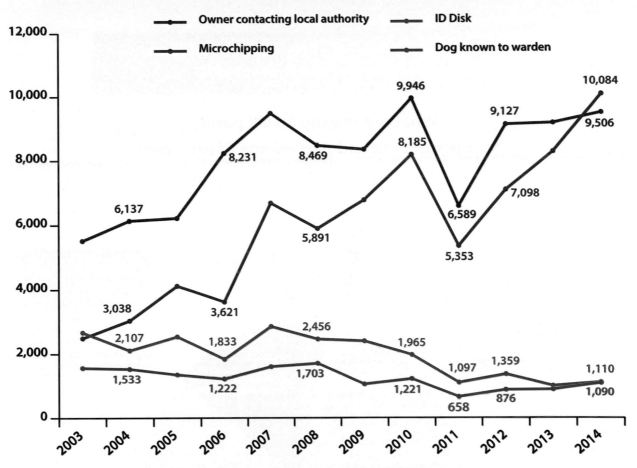

*A combination of microchip and ID collar accounted for a further **882** reunions.
Other reasons dogs were able to be returned to their owners included the dog having a collar - **206 dogs**, or the dog having an identifying tattoo - **55 dogs**. Information was not available or had not been kept for **2,706 dogs**.

MISSING

REWARD FOR SAFE RETURN

New figures from Dogs Trust also show that traditional means of trying to find a missing dog are largely ineffective. **50%** of those surveyed said when they see a missing dog poster, they never take any action to note down the contact information or details.

35% of dogs were reclaimed during the seven day period local authorities will keep dogs and **15%** were returned directly to their owner without entering a kennel.

Some issues

- Will microchipping all dogs solve this problem?
- Should there be some restriction on who can own a dog?
- What would be the best action to take to find a missing dog?
- If a stray is rehomed and the original owner wants it back, what should be done?

Base: 359 UK local authorities responded to the 2014 Stray Dog Survey by GfK NOP and a separate survey of 1,000 UK-based dog owners was carried out by OnePoll on behalf of the Dogs Trust.

Source: Dogs Trust www.dogstrust.org.uk

Pet population

There are 65 million pets in the UK, but which are the most popular?

In 2014 it was estimated that around **46% of households** have pets - this is about **13 million households.**

What are the top 10 UK pets?
Number of pets and percentage of total pets

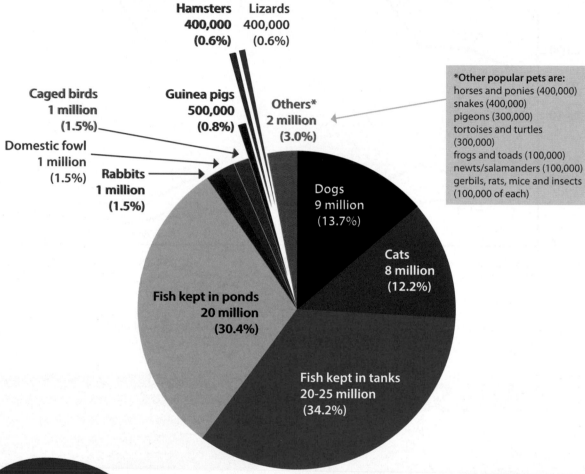

Hamsters
**400,000
(0.6%)**

Lizards
**400,000
(0.6%)**

Caged birds
**1 million
(1.5%)**

Domestic fowl
**1 million
(1.5%)**

Rabbits
**1 million
(1.5%)**

Guinea pigs
**500,000
(0.8%)**

Others*
**2 million
(3.0%)**

*Other popular pets are:
horses and ponies (400,000)
snakes (400,000)
pigeons (300,000)
tortoises and turtles
(300,000)
frogs and toads (100,000)
newts/salamanders (100,000)
gerbils, rats, mice and insects
(100,000 of each)

Dogs
**9 million
(13.7%)**

Cats
**8 million
(12.2%)**

Fish kept in ponds
**20 million
(30.4%)**

Fish kept in tanks
**20-25 million
(34.2%)**

Some issues

- What are the attractions of exotic pets like lizards?

- Many people regard pets as friends and companions. Is this just wishful thinking?

- What are the advantages of having a pet?

Base: Estimates of the UK pet population were made over two years using a total sample of 6,000 people.

*Source: TNS research for Pet Food Manufacturers' Association PFMA
www.pfma.org.uk/pet-population-2014*

Art &
culture

Culture fix

Are we taking part in fewer cultural activities... or just changing how we are experiencing them?

Nearly 27,000 people across the EU were interviewed for the Cultural Access and Participation survey.

Which of the following activities have you done at least once over the past 12 months?

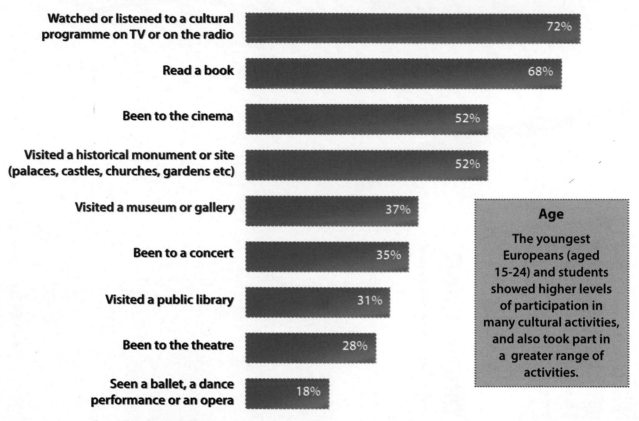

Activity	%
Watched or listened to a cultural programme on TV or on the radio	72%
Read a book	68%
Been to the cinema	52%
Visited a historical monument or site (palaces, castles, churches, gardens etc)	52%
Visited a museum or gallery	37%
Been to a concert	35%
Visited a public library	31%
Been to the theatre	28%
Seen a ballet, a dance performance or an opera	18%

Age

The youngest Europeans (aged 15-24) and students showed higher levels of participation in many cultural activities, and also took part in a greater range of activities.

Barriers to accessing cultural activities

People said that lack of interest or lack of time were the main obstacles to participating in a particular activity. Lack of interest was the main reason for not going to more concerts (29%), visiting a museum or gallery (35%), going to the theatre (36%), visiting a public library (43%) or attending a ballet, dance performance or opera (50%).

Lack of time was the main reason for not going to the cinema (30%), watching or listening to a cultural programme on the TV or radio (31%), visiting a historical monument or site (37%), or reading a book (44%).

Internet

The internet is changing the way people access cultural content and its influence is increasing in importance for everyone.

The survey showed that **56%** of Europeans use the internet for cultural purposes - **30%** doing so at least once a week.

What cultural activity do you use the internet for?

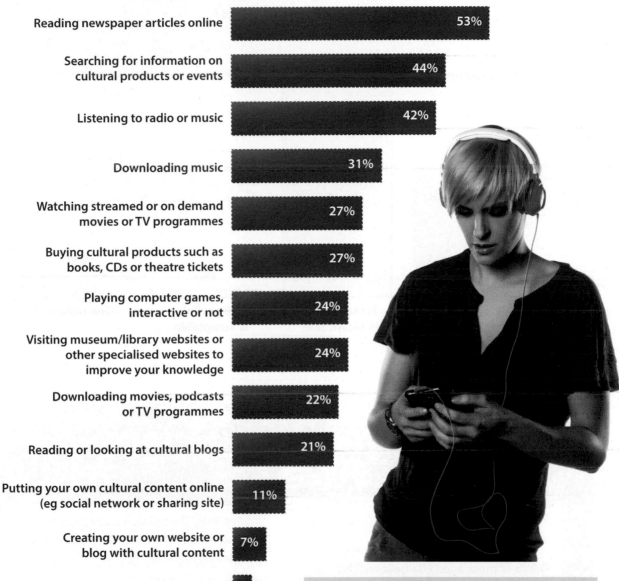

Activity	Percentage
Reading newspaper articles online	53%
Searching for information on cultural products or events	44%
Listening to radio or music	42%
Downloading music	31%
Watching streamed or on demand movies or TV programmes	27%
Buying cultural products such as books, CDs or theatre tickets	27%
Playing computer games, interactive or not	24%
Visiting museum/library websites or other specialised websites to improve your knowledge	24%
Downloading movies, podcasts or TV programmes	22%
Reading or looking at cultural blogs	21%
Putting your own cultural content online (eg social network or sharing site)	11%
Creating your own website or blog with cultural content	7%
Other	4%
Don't know	2%

80% of people in Denmark, **78%** of people in Sweden and **77%** of Estonians said reading newspaper articles online was their main use of the internet for cultural purposes.

Downloading music was the main answer in Greece (**60%**) and Bulgaria (**45%**), and the second most common use in Cyprus (**61%**).

Some issues

- Will the internet discourage people from going to 'live' cultural events or venues?

- Should people be encouraged to take more interest in culture?

- Why do you think more young people are involved in cultural activities?

- Are there any other factors which stop people taking part in cultural activities?

Source: Cultural Access and Participation survey 2013, European Commission
http://europa.eu

Graffiti

Certain types of people appreciate graffiti as an artform while others think it is vandalism

Thinking about graffiti which of these best reflects your views?

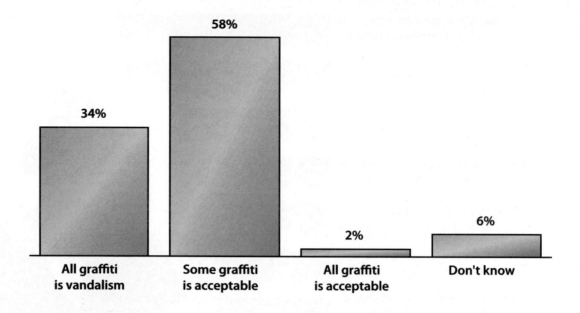

- All graffiti is vandalism — 34%
- Some graffiti is acceptable — 58%
- All graffiti is acceptable — 2%
- Don't know — 6%

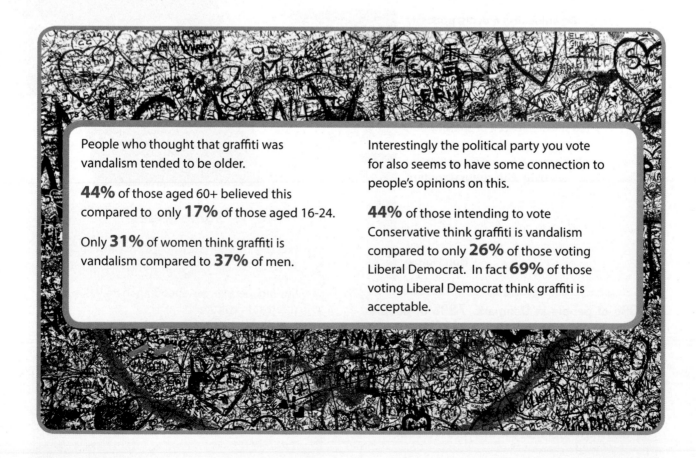

People who thought that graffiti was vandalism tended to be older.

44% of those aged 60+ believed this compared to only **17%** of those aged 16-24.

Only **31%** of women think graffiti is vandalism compared to **37%** of men.

Interestingly the political party you vote for also seems to have some connection to people's opinions on this.

44% of those intending to vote Conservative think graffiti is vandalism compared to only **26%** of those voting Liberal Democrat. In fact **69%** of those voting Liberal Democrat think graffiti is acceptable.

Do you think graffiti can be considered as "art"?

(Figures do not add up to 100% due to rounding)

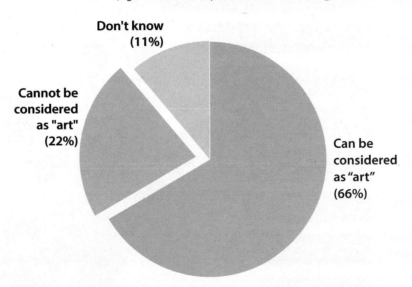

Don't know
(11%)

Cannot be
considered
as "art"
(22%)

Can be
considered
as "art"
(66%)

Those who think that graffiti can be considered as "art" tend also to be younger and female. **75%** of those aged 16-24 and 25-39 think that graffiti should be considered as "art". Only **65%** of those aged 40-59 and **56%** of those aged 60+ agree with this opinion.

61% of men but **71%** of women think that graffiti can be considered as "art".

Where you live also seems to affect your opinion on graffiti. **71%** of those from the Midlands and Wales agree that it is art while only **60%** of Scots share this point of view.

Some issues

- Do you like graffiti? And do you consider it as art?

- Why do you think there is a difference between gender and age group as to who likes or dislikes graffiti?

- Who should decide whether graffiti should be removed or not?

- What factors should be considered when making this decision?

Base: Survey of 1,649 GB adults

Source: Yougov www.yougov.co.uk

Visitor attractions

The most popular places to visit

Number of visits made to visitor attractions in 2013 - Top twenty locations

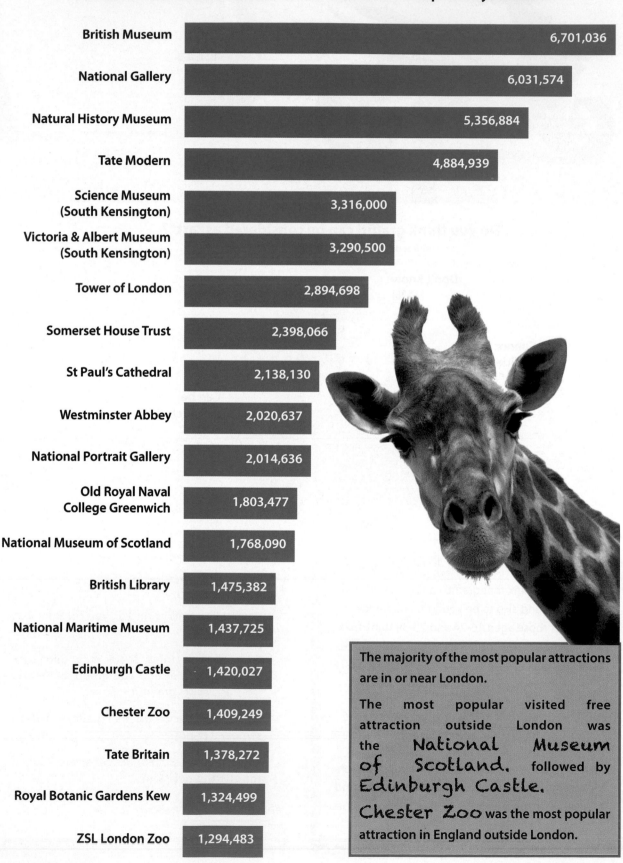

British Museum	6,701,036
National Gallery	6,031,574
Natural History Museum	5,356,884
Tate Modern	4,884,939
Science Museum (South Kensington)	3,316,000
Victoria & Albert Museum (South Kensington)	3,290,500
Tower of London	2,894,698
Somerset House Trust	2,398,066
St Paul's Cathedral	2,138,130
Westminster Abbey	2,020,637
National Portrait Gallery	2,014,636
Old Royal Naval College Greenwich	1,803,477
National Museum of Scotland	1,768,090
British Library	1,475,382
National Maritime Museum	1,437,725
Edinburgh Castle	1,420,027
Chester Zoo	1,409,249
Tate Britain	1,378,272
Royal Botanic Gardens Kew	1,324,499
ZSL London Zoo	1,294,483

The majority of the most popular attractions are in or near London.

The most popular visited free attraction outside London was the National Museum of Scotland, followed by Edinburgh Castle. Chester Zoo was the most popular attraction in England outside London.

There was an average increase of **6%** on 2012 visitor numbers over all attractions.

The **British Museum** was the most popular for the 7th year running with a **20%** increase in visitor numbers. 2013 was its most successful year on record.

The newly opened Library of Birmingham had **1,152,556** visitors in just four months.

Visitors to the **National Gallery** rose by **14%** and visitors to the **Natural History Museum** rose by **6.7%**.

The opening of the **Mary Rose Museum** at Portsmouth Historic Dockyard brought in **674,434** visitors - up **55%**, the highest rise in visitor figures.

Photo: Library of Birmingham
© bjonesphotography

"Last year was another record breaking one for the Natural History Museum... it shows the continued success of the free admission policy and the public's real interest in science and environmental issues"

Dr Michael Dixon
Director of Natural History Museum

Some issues

- Why do you think some attractions have more visitors than others?

- Why do you think more places outside of London do not feature?

- Should people from other parts of the country get special help to visit these top attractions?

- How can people be encouraged to visit places outside London?

- What is your favourite museum or gallery?

Source: ALVA Association of Leading Visitor Attractions
www.alva.org.uk/details.cfm?p=604

Museums at night

Visitor numbers show that people can't get enough of Britain's museums

Museums at Night is an annual UK-wide festival which encourages visitors into museums, galleries and heritage sites by opening after hours and putting on special evening events.

In 2013:

411
arts and heritage venues opened their doors at night

583
events took place

200
UK towns hosted events

145,841
visits were made to events

4,375 visits
were made by people who had never been to an arts or heritage venue prior to Museums at Night.
This was **3%** of all visits

42,294 visits
were made by people new to the venue they visited.
This was **29%** of all visits

97%
of visitors rated their experience as
7 out of 10 or more

97%
of visitors were inspired to visit other heritage and arts venues

£1.65m
spent by visitors on other items such as food, drink and travel

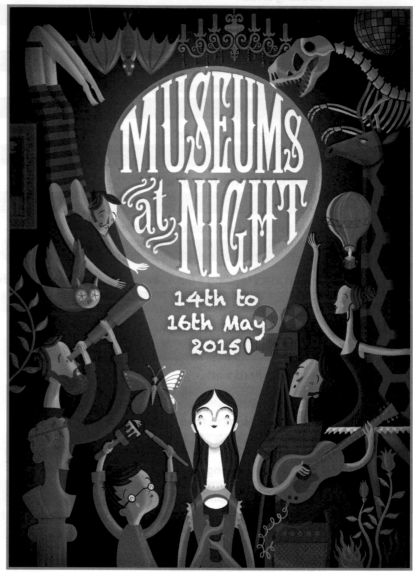

MUSEUMS at NIGHT
14th to 16th May 2015

© Stuart Kolakovic

Some issues

- Why hasn't the internet dampened people's appetite for museums?
- How important is it that there is free admission to museums?
- What special features make museums interesting?
- Why is this special event important?

Source: Museums at Night
www.museumsatnight.org.uk

Body
image

Body issues

The media pressures young girls to conform to gender stereotypes

Girlguiding is the leading charity for girls and young women in the UK. Girlguiding's fifth Girls' Attitudes Survey provides a unique overview of the issues facing girls aged 7 to 21 in the UK today facing girls in the UK today.

Gender norms

By the time girls reach secondary school **90%** are taking conscious steps to make their appearance conform to accepted gender norms. This is clearly influenced by the media and advertising. In many cases this leads to girls spending substantial sums of money on beauty products.

Spray tan/
use tanning
products

34%

64%
Wear make-
up to school

40%
Wear a
padded bra

20%

9%
None of
these

**Wear
revealing or
fashionable clothes
they find
uncomfortable**

77%
Shave or wax
their legs

27%

Alter school uniform
to be shorter or
tighter

**Changes
girls make
to their
appearance
(11 to 16)**

21%

have tried a
celebrity diet
(11 to 21)

Pressure to conform to an idealised body
size starts early in girls' lives and increases
as they progress through their teens.
Overall, **71%** of 11- to 21–year-olds say
that they would like to lose weight.

20%

48%

56%

7 to 11

11 to 16

16 to 21

Girls
who say
they have
been on a
diet

'An equal society is one where
people are not judged for their
appearance, everyone has an equal
right to education, everyone has the
ability to follow their chosen career
path, everyone has a right to a voice
and opinion, and men and women
are treated equally.'
Guide, 14

Some issues

- What is influencing such young women to diet?

- Are there similar changes that boys feel
  compelled to make to their appearance?

- What can be done to encourage a more positive
  body image in young girls?

Source: Equality for Girls, Girls' Attitudes survey 2013
www.girlguiding.org.uk

Looking good

How much do men and women worry about their looks?

Women feel twice as much pressure to look good than men do...

Women

66% of the women felt under too much pressure to look good, saying that the rise in 'perfect-looking' women in the media set unrealistic standards.

60% of women go as far as to say they get anxious about their image.

Women are also **twice as likely** to feel scrutinised for their appearance at work as men and experienced more bouts of feeling self-conscious about their body on holiday, at parties and even just at home.

Top five body worries for women

- weight
- teeth
- cellulite
- bags under the eyes
- fear of having flabby arms or 'bingo wings'

"...body hang-ups can have an effect on people of all shapes, sizes and genders – whether it relates to weight, body shape or clothing, both men and women can feel at times under pressure to live up to 'expectation'."

Helen Smith, Head of Research at Benenden Health

...but the pressure is growing on men as they feel the level of expectation placed upon them is rising

Men

The survey showed that there was a rise in men dressing for their body shape, discussing their image with partners and **over 12%** of men were even dieting in secret.

Men were worried they would be judged by other male friends for showing too much concern about their health and image.

They were concerned that it wasn't 'blokey' to show they were bothered about the way they looked.

Top five body worries for men

- **58%** were anxious about being overweight or having a beer belly

- **20%** said yellowing teeth

- **14%** were concerned over a lack of muscle

- **19.2%** worried over balding or receding hair lines

- **19.4%** said man boobs or 'moobs'

These rising levels of worry led **75%** of men to think they were pressured to meet high standards of appearance far more than generations before them ever were.

In another survey, it was found that **men** gave up on their health and appearance at the **age of 46** while **women** were **59** before they 'relaxed their standards'.

In later years, maintaining physical wellbeing became less of a priority. People prefer to relax in comfort and not have to keep up with trends.

66% thought it was normal to give up on worrying about appearance once someone had a serious partner.

Some issues

- Why do you think people are so concerned about the way they look?

- Why do you think men are embarrassed to be concerned about their appearance?

- Why does this issue affect more women than men?

Base: Both surveys questioned 2,000 men and women

Source: Benenden Health, 2014 www.benenden.co.uk

Cosmetic surgery

People seem keen to alter their appearance – especially women

There were **50,122** surgical procedures carried out in 2013,
a rise of **16.5%** on average overall since 2012.
No procedures decreased in popularity.

The top surgical procedures for men and women, 2013
(Number of procedures)

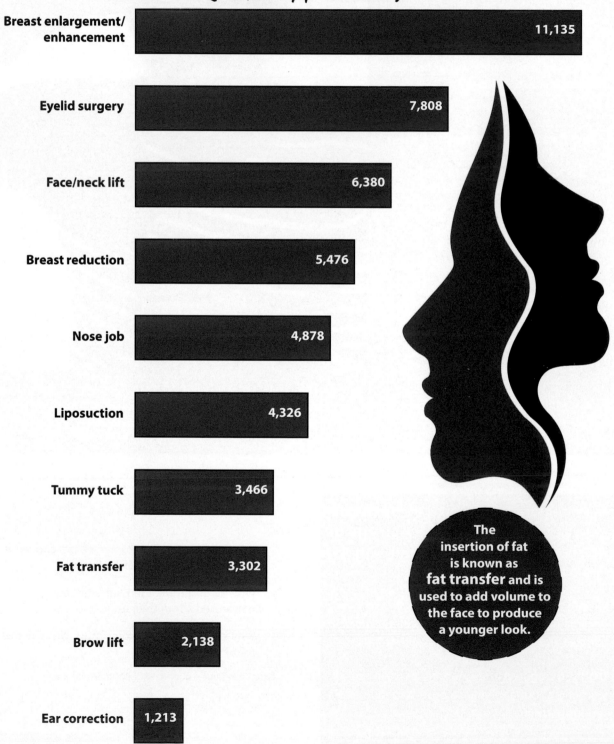

Procedure	Number
Breast enlargement/enhancement	11,135
Eyelid surgery	7,808
Face/neck lift	6,380
Breast reduction	5,476
Nose job	4,878
Liposuction	4,326
Tummy tuck	3,466
Fat transfer	3,302
Brow lift	2,138
Ear correction	1,213

The insertion of fat is known as **fat transfer** and is used to add volume to the face to produce a younger look.

Women had 45,365 procedures: 90.5% of all cosmetic procedures in 2013

Top ten procedures (in order of popularity)	Number of procedures	% rise or fall from 2011
Breast enlargement/ enhancement	11,123	+13%
Eyelid surgery	6,921	+14%
Face/neck lift	6,016	+13%
Breast reduction	4,680	+11%
Nose job	3,841	+19%
Liposuction	3,772	+43%
Tummy tuck	3,343	+16%
Fat transfer	3,037	+15%
Brow lift	1,962	+18%
Ear correction	670	+19%

Men had 4,757 procedures: 9.5% of all cosmetic procedures in 2013

Top ten procedures (in order of popularity)	Number of procedures	% rise or fall from 2011
Nose job	1,037	+9%
Eyelid surgery	887	+17%
Breast reduction	796	+24%
Liposuction	554	+28%
Ear correction	543	+8%
Face/neck lift	364	+19%
Fat transfer	265	+10%
Brow lift	176	+18%
Tummy tuck	123	+15%
Breast enlargement/ enhancement	12	no change

The cost of fashion

In 2014, cosmetic surgeons reported a big increase in repairs to earlobes stretched by tribal ear piercing (flesh tunnels) - this surgery can cost around **£1,800.**

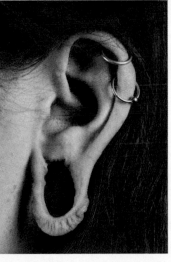

Some issues

- Is it a good thing that people want to look younger?

- Do the benefits really outweigh the risks?

- Why do so many more women than men have cosmetic surgery?

- Should all cosmetic procedures be paid for by the patient or should some be free?

Source: British Association of Aesthetic Plastic Surgeons www.baaps.org.uk

Body art

Views on tattoos

What you need to know about tattoos

- A tattoo is a permanent design using coloured ink pigment punctured deep into the skin.

- Some find the pain hard to cope with. Others think it's an important part of the process.

- If you're under 18 it's ILLEGAL to get a tattoo.

- Tattoos must be performed by professional tattooists under totally hygienic conditions.

- To avoid the risk of infections like tetanus or even HIV, the tattooist must use a new needle and tube from a sealed packet, and the ink should be in disposable pots.

An online survey of 2,009 UK adults revealed that **23%** of those surveyed had a tattoo, with similar numbers of males as females having one - **13%** had more than one.

Those who didn't have a tattoo were asked their reasons for NOT getting one
(more than one answer could be given)

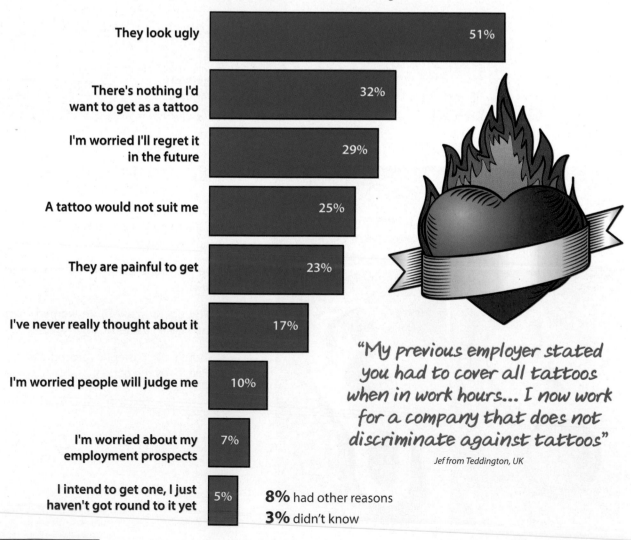

They look ugly	51%
There's nothing I'd want to get as a tattoo	32%
I'm worried I'll regret it in the future	29%
A tattoo would not suit me	25%
They are painful to get	23%
I've never really thought about it	17%
I'm worried people will judge me	10%
I'm worried about my employment prospects	7%
I intend to get one, I just haven't got round to it yet	5%

8% had other reasons
3% didn't know

"My previous employer stated you had to cover all tattoos when in work hours... I now work for a company that does not discriminate against tattoos"

Jef from Teddington, UK

Those that did have tattoos were asked their reasons for getting one

(more than one answer could be given)

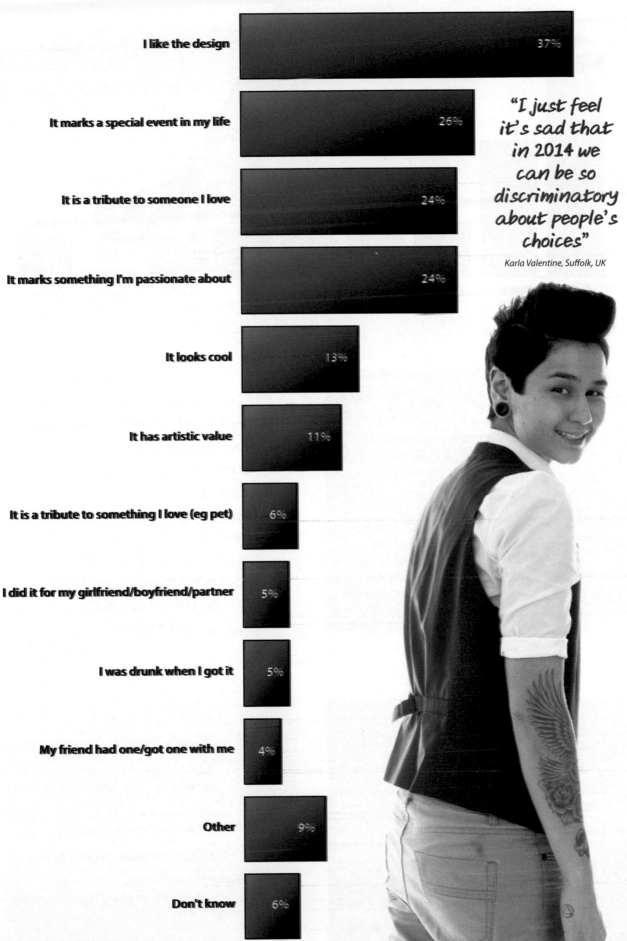

Reason	Percentage
I like the design	37%
It marks a special event in my life	26%
It is a tribute to someone I love	24%
It marks something I'm passionate about	24%
It looks cool	13%
It has artistic value	11%
It is a tribute to something I love (eg pet)	6%
I did it for my girlfriend/boyfriend/partner	5%
I was drunk when I got it	5%
My friend had one/got one with me	4%
Other	9%
Don't know	6%

> "I just feel it's sad that in 2014 we can be so discriminatory about people's choices"
>
> Karla Valentine, Suffolk, UK

Photo posed by model

Those that did have a tattoo were asked which of their body parts was tattooed

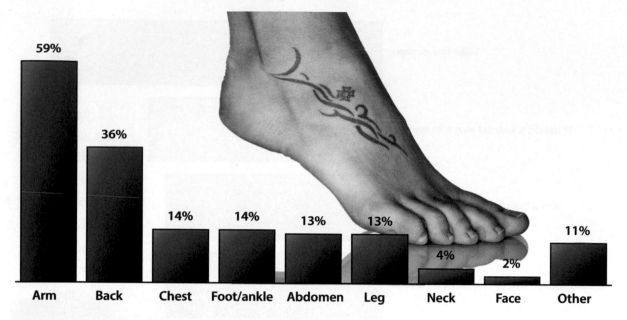

59%	36%	14%	14%	13%	13%	4%	2%	11%
Arm	Back	Chest	Foot/ankle	Abdomen	Leg	Neck	Face	Other

Did the clothes they wore out in public or at work make their tattoos visible to others?

32% said at least one of their tattoos was visible when they were **out in public**

19% said at least one of their tattoos was visible when they were **at work**

60% said their tattoos were not in a visible place when **at work** or **out in public**

1% preferred not to say

NB The base is small for those who did have tattoos

"I've had very mixed reactions to my art... people either love them and find me brave or hate me and insult me... I'm not rude or horrible... I work hard, pay bills, do charity work for animals... Just cause I'm heavily tattooed doesn't mean I'm nasty, scary or stupid."

Amii Parr, Reading, UK

Advice from The Site - If you decide to have a tattoo:

- You should know exactly what design you want and where.

- You should talk to the tattooist, then go away and think about it.

- Before getting tattooed, you should be aware that if you ever want it removed it would involve ultrasound treatment, which can be expensive.

- You should always follow the tattooist's advice about after care.

Some issues

- How long should you think about it before you get a tattoo?

- Why are people sometimes prejudiced against tattoos?

- Why have tattoos become so popular?

- Why might some people regret having a tattoo?

See also: *Just one little tattoo, Essential Articles 2015, p66*

Source: Opinium Research www.opinium.co.uk The Site www.thesite.org BBC Magazine www.bbc.co.uk/news/magazine-29211526

Britain & its citizens

As others see us

What people from other countries think about the UK

Over 5,000 18-34 year olds from Brazil, China, Germany, India and US were asked*

Which, if any, of the following characteristics make the UK ATTRACTIVE?
(more than one answer could be given)

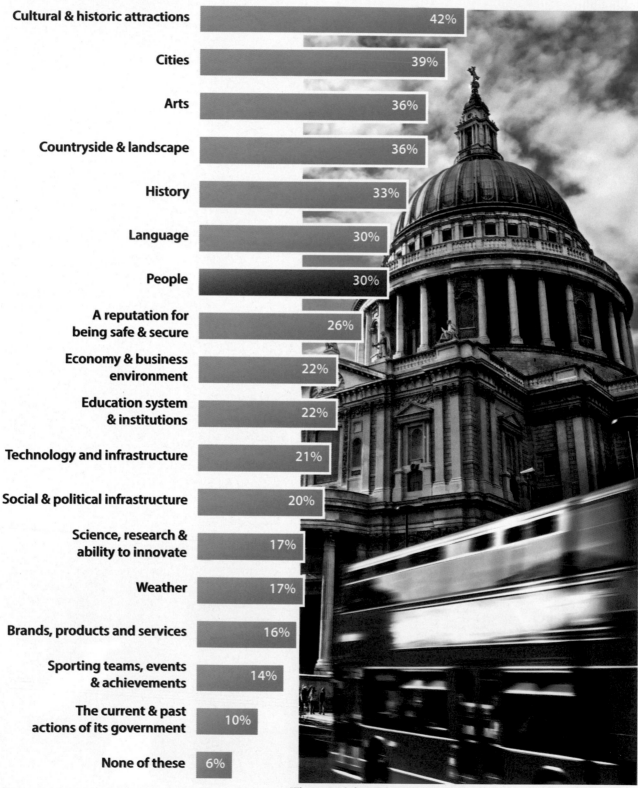

Characteristic	Percentage
Cultural & historic attractions	42%
Cities	39%
Arts	36%
Countryside & landscape	36%
History	33%
Language	30%
People	30%
A reputation for being safe & secure	26%
Economy & business environment	22%
Education system & institutions	22%
Technology and infrastructure	21%
Social & political infrastructure	20%
Science, research & ability to innovate	17%
Weather	17%
Brands, products and services	16%
Sporting teams, events & achievements	14%
The current & past actions of its government	10%
None of these	6%

*The research focused on young educated people in countries with whom the UK is seeking to connect for education, tourism and/or business purposes.

It probably isn't surprising that **the weather, climate and cold** were frequently mentioned, but the UK's **people** were also mentioned as an **unattractive** feature.

This is interesting, as previous studies suggested that people from the UK are often seen as tolerant, diverse, broad-minded and open to new ideas.

Of course, people generally, and individuals in particular, can have both positive and negative qualities. Views about people are often based on personal experience and so it is not unusual to have both positive and negative views of national populations at the same time.

Overall, when it comes to the attractiveness of its people in general, the UK comes second only to the US.

Which do you think are the BEST characteristics of people in the UK?

(respondents could choose three)

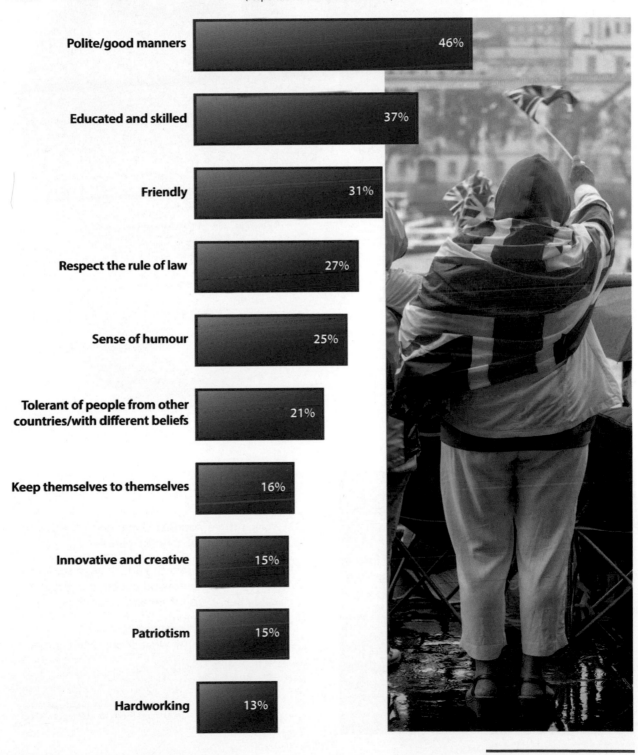

Characteristic	%
Polite/good manners	46%
Educated and skilled	37%
Friendly	31%
Respect the rule of law	27%
Sense of humour	25%
Tolerant of people from other countries/with different beliefs	21%
Keep themselves to themselves	16%
Innovative and creative	15%
Patriotism	15%
Hardworking	13%

Which three, if any, do you think are the WORST characteristics of people in the UK?

(respondents could choose three)

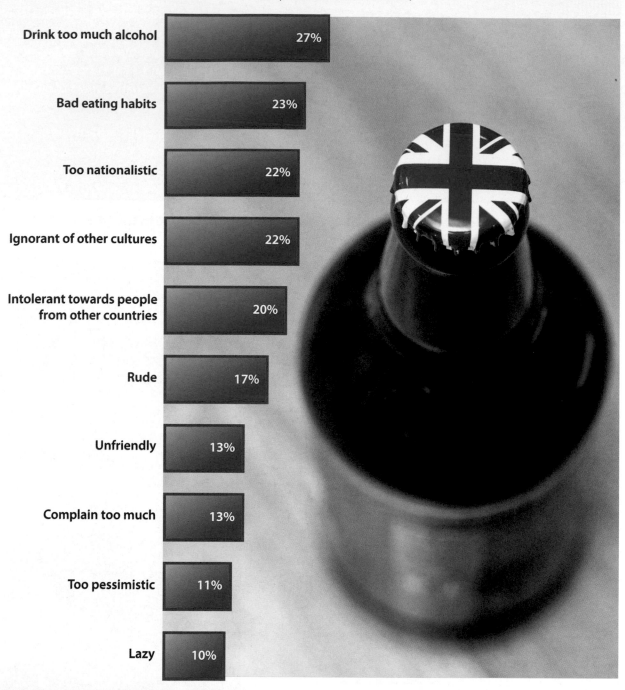

Characteristic	%
Drink too much alcohol	27%
Bad eating habits	23%
Too nationalistic	22%
Ignorant of other cultures	22%
Intolerant towards people from other countries	20%
Rude	17%
Unfriendly	13%
Complain too much	13%
Too pessimistic	11%
Lazy	10%

British reputation abroad

Personal experience of the UK influenced people's opinions.

For example, **34%** of those who **had been** to the UK concluded that we drank too much alcohol compared to **24%** who **had not been** to the UK.

Only **16%** of those who **had been** to the UK, thought we were **intolerant** compared to **21%** who **had not been** to the UK.

Some issues

- Which three national characteristics do you think are typical of British people?

- 21% of people said the British were **tolerant** towards people from other countries yet 20% said they were **intolerant**. In your opinion, which is nearer to the truth?

- Why does it matter what people from abroad think of our nation?

Source: Research by Ipsos MORI and In2Impact for the British Council - As Others See Us www.britishcouncil.org

Role models

Two surveys of 2,001 UK adults aged 18+ revealed how we
view the relationship between fame and being a role model

63% of those questioned think being a public figure automatically makes you a potential role model.

55% agreed it was the duty of the rich and famous to use their influence for good (eg raising money for a good cause).

35% said that celebrities should not be expected to worry about who they socialise with, even in public.

52% said that celebrities are more likely to be known for their beauty rather than their achievements.

51% thought it was unreasonable to expect celebrities to be able to always control how their personal image is used by the media and the public.

79% thought that if celebrities actively seek the attention of the media they should accept that people will probe what they say and do.

71% thought celebrities needed to be more careful than others about the brands they promoted or recommended.

Scarlett Johansson
Photo: © ChinelatoPhoto

Scarlett Johansson caused controversy with Oxfam in 2014. They considered that her role of promoting the company SodaStream was incompatible with her role as an Oxfam Global Ambassador.

Oxfam are opposed to all trade from Israeli settlements, which are illegal under international law and said:

"Oxfam believes that businesses, such as SodaStream, that operate in settlements further the ongoing poverty and denial of rights of the Palestinian communities that we work to support."

Scarlett Johansson said:

"I don't see myself as being a role model. I never wanted to step into those shoes.

I don't profess to know more or less than anybody else. If that's a by-product of whatever image is projected on to me I don't feel responsible as an artist to give anyone that message."

Q. From a list of celebrities and other people in the spotlight, who, if any, would you say sets a GOOD example? (Top ten people chosen)

34% David Attenborough
30% Prince William
27% The Queen
25% Richard Branson
24% David Beckham
22% Joanna Lumley
22% Catherine, Duchess of Cambridge
20% Bill Gates
19% Prince Harry
18% Stephen Fry

21% said none of those mentioned

The Duke and Duchess of Cambridge both appear in the top 10
Photo: © Shaun Jeffers

Other people mentioned were: Gary Barlow, Jamie Oliver, Davina McCall, Cliff Richard, Katie Piper, Holly Willoughby, Angelina Jolie, Peter Andre, Boris Johnson, Jeremy Clarkson

Q. ...And who, if any, would you say sets a BAD example? (Top ten people chosen)

56% Justin Bieber
45% Katie Price
45% Russell Brand
41% Miley Cyrus
38% Lindsey Lohan
34% Max Clifford
30% Wayne Rooney
29% John Terry
29% Lady Gaga
28% Tony Blair

12% said none of those mentioned

Justin Bieber
Photo: © JStone

Miley Cyrus
Photo: © JStone

Other people mentioned were: Jeremy Clarkson, Jonathan Ross, Piers Morgan, Rihanna, David Cameron, Kate Moss, Nick Clegg, Ed Balls, Boris Johnson

Q. Thinking about specific people you look up to as a good example to follow, which of the following, if any, would you say are role models for you?

Your parent(s)	35%
A friend	19%
Other relative(s)	10%
Your sibling(s)	10%
A teacher/lecturer	10%
Someone in my profession or workplace	9%
Someone in the emergency services (eg police, fire)	7%
Religious figure	6%
Someone in the armed forces	6%
Someone in the local community	5%
Other (including musician/band, politician, actor/actress/other celebrity)	13%
None of the above	34%

70% thought that unlike ordinary people, celebrities need to consider how their behaviour influences and affects others.

81% thought young people needed more role models who weren't celebrities.

Just **14%** said they would like to be famous one day.

Some issues

- Four members of the Royal family appear in the top 10 good examples - why do you think this is?

- Can you explain why some people appeared in both the good AND bad list?

- Do you think that being in the limelight automatically makes a person a role model?

- Why should a person in the limelight be considered a role model?

- Do young people need role models at all?

Source: Opinium Research **www.opinium.co.uk**

Political participation

Political engagement, by age

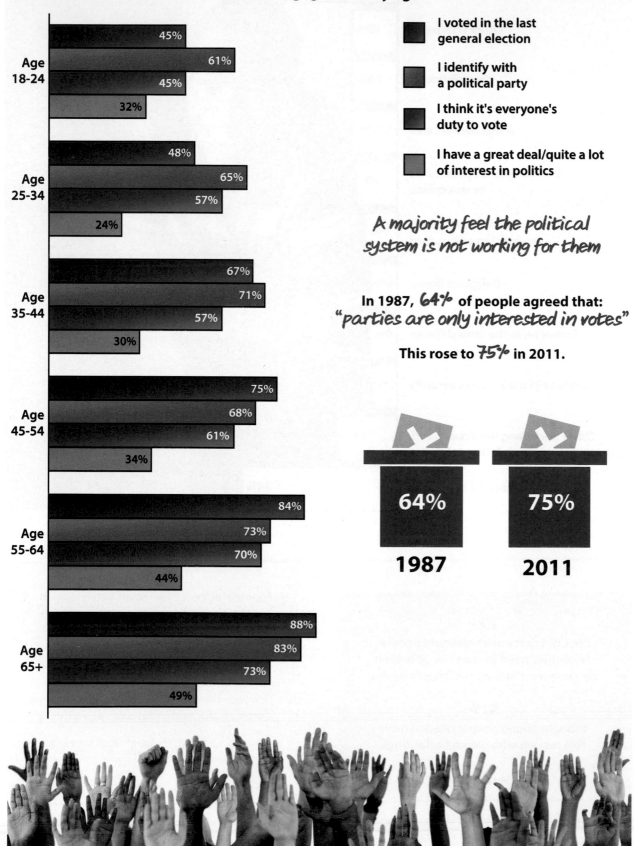

Legend:
- I voted in the last general election
- I identify with a political party
- I think it's everyone's duty to vote
- I have a great deal/quite a lot of interest in politics

Age 18-24
- 45%
- 61%
- 45%
- 32%

Age 25-34
- 48%
- 65%
- 57%
- 24%

Age 35-44
- 67%
- 71%
- 57%
- 30%

Age 45-54
- 75%
- 68%
- 61%
- 34%

Age 55-64
- 84%
- 73%
- 70%
- 44%

Age 65+
- 88%
- 83%
- 73%
- 49%

A majority feel the political system is not working for them

In 1987, **64%** of people agreed that: *"parties are only interested in votes"*

This rose to **75%** in 2011.

64% — **1987**

75% — **2011**

Younger people are less politically interested than in the past

In 1983, *85%* of those in their 20s or early 30s identified with a particular political party.

In 2012, this had fallen to *66%* of the same age group.

1983 **2012**

How have you taken part in political activity?

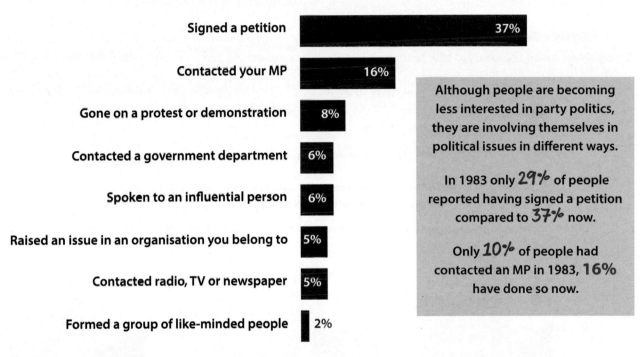

Signed a petition	37%
Contacted your MP	16%
Gone on a protest or demonstration	8%
Contacted a government department	6%
Spoken to an influential person	6%
Raised an issue in an organisation you belong to	5%
Contacted radio, TV or newspaper	5%
Formed a group of like-minded people	2%

Lastest figures, 2011

Although people are becoming less interested in party politics, they are involving themselves in political issues in different ways.

In 1983 only *29%* of people reported having signed a petition compared to *37%* now.

Only *10%* of people had contacted an MP in 1983, **16%** have done so now.

More highly educated people remain more engaged with politics

52% of people with a degree are interested in politics compared to *24%* of those without any qualifications.

77% of those with a degree think it is everybody's duty to vote compared to *56%* of people without any formal qualifications.

In fact *77%* of people without qualifications think that politics is too complicated to understand compared to *38%* with a degree.

Some issues

- Why are young people losing interest in politics?

- What action can you take if you believe that something needs to be changed in our national life?

- What issues would make you take action?

Source: British Social Attitudes 30 www.natcen.ac.uk

Small talk

How people feel about talking to their neighbours

Small talk (polite chat about things that aren't very important) with neighbours didn't come naturally for almost half of those questioned, but around 66% of people said it made them feel happier.

60% of adults make small talk with their neighbours and 52% even went out of their way to start a conversation;

20% said they didn't feel comfortable making small talk with their neighbours;

21% said they were flattered by the interest when a neighbour made the effort to talk to them;

Over 25% said it made them feel that they mattered and were less invisible;

For more than 5%, talking with a neighbour was one of the highlights of their day;

70% of those who made small talk claimed that a simple conversation with a neighbour made them feel more in touch with the rest of their community.

72% of over 55s said small talk came naturally compared to just 35% of under 35s.

20% of under 25s said that they DID NOT talk AT ALL to their neighbours.

Where small talk happens

The garden was the top location for small talk - whether hanging out the washing, washing the car or other outdoor chores.

Bumping into neighbours in the local shops or pub also provides small talk meeting points.

34% of those questioned said that the simple act of talking to your neighbour was a way to 'brighten someone's day';

30% considered it a 'lifeline' for those who lived alone;

53% of those surveyed admitted they had at least one neighbour they had NEVER said 'hello' or 'good morning' to;

5% said they have never engaged in small talk with a neighbour, while another **5%** admitted it had been years.

Over **40%** claimed they wished they had a better relationship with the people living around them, while only **10%** said they were firm friends with the person living next door.

Why people speak to neighbours

33% said they wanted to talk about something that happened locally, while around **12%** used small talk as a means to an end - eg asking their neighbour for a favour.

Why people hold back from talking to neighbours

36% said they didn't know what to say;

29% said shyness;

22% said lack of time.

Top ten small talk subjects

- **Weather**
- **Holidays**
- **Enquiring about well-being**
- **Your/their children**
- **Local events happening in the community**
- **Gossip or news about other neighbours**
- **Work**
- **National news/current affairs**
- **Traffic**
- **Crime levels in the area**

Some issues

- Should people chat more?

- What reasons are there for the difference between generations when it comes to talking to neighbours?

- Is being able to make small talk an important skill?

- Why is small talk good for people?

- Why do people choose topics that are not controversial for this kind of chat?

Source: Study of 2,000 British adults by The Big Lunch
www.thebiglunch.com

Giving thanks

Attitudes and thoughts on saying thank you in the modern world

There is still a strong demand for people to express their thanks in the UK: **93%** of people agree that receiving a thank you brightens up their day. **80%** admitted they are more likely to help people who say thank you.

The way we thank people has changed over the years:

Modern day methods

Social media | 35%

Email | 65%

Emoticon | 22%

"...whilst saying thank you on these platforms is better than not saying it at all, saying it face-to-face has much more of an impact."

Professor Cary Cooper CBE,
Professor of Organisational Psychology and Health,
Lancaster University

Traditional method

Thank you letter | 18%

60% of us think that we say thank you less than we used to
80% of us believe we don't say it enough!

People who are most likely to say thanks if you do them a favour

- Friends — 63%
- Colleagues — 60%
- Parents — 44%
- Siblings — 27%
- Other family members — 25%

15% said thank you between **50 and 100 times a day,** with the average Brit saying it **32 times**

The more traditional ways of saying thank you were most popular generally:

Thank you
Thanks
Cheers

Those in England & Wales preferred:

Nice one
Wicked

Those in Scotland preferred:

Cheers
Great

Most popular ways of saying thanks:

71% chose flowers

60% chose a hug

Nearly **85%** rated saying thank you as very important

70% thought **young people** don't say thank you enough

Some issues

- How do you feel when someone doesn't thank you for something?
- Is it true that young people don't say thank you enough?
- How important is the way you thank someone?
- What is the best way to thank someone?

Source: Mission Thank You survey by Cash For Kids
www.cashforkids.uk.com

Base: 6,614 UK adults

Phobias

What are you afraid of?

http://yougov.co.uk

Are you afraid of any of the following things?

(Base 2,088 GB adults - figures do not add up to 100% due to rounding)

■ Very afraid   ■ A little afraid

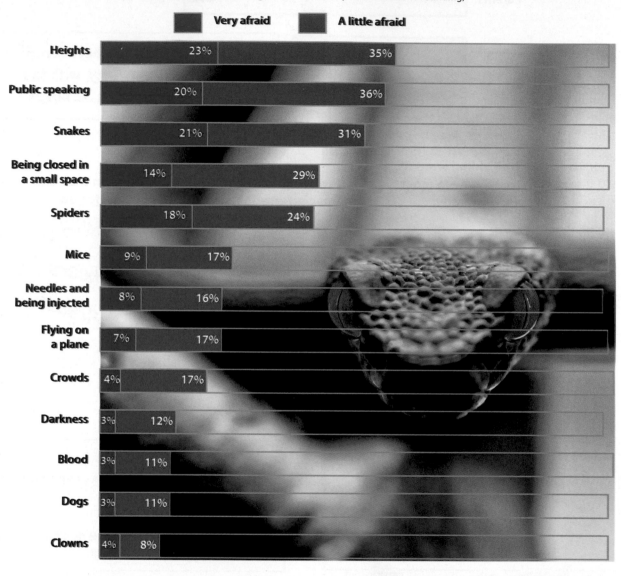

	Very afraid	A little afraid
Heights	23%	35%
Public speaking	20%	36%
Snakes	21%	31%
Being closed in a small space	14%	29%
Spiders	18%	24%
Mice	9%	17%
Needles and being injected	8%	16%
Flying on a plane	7%	17%
Crowds	4%	17%
Darkness	3%	12%
Blood	3%	11%
Dogs	3%	11%
Clowns	4%	8%

Gender and generation gaps

More women than men are afraid of each of the fears listed, but men and women seem equally afraid of needles/injections and blood.

The gender gap is widest when it comes to spiders, which scare **33%** of men and **52%** of women.

Younger people were more likely to be afraid of public speaking but older age groups were more likely than younger people to be afraid of heights and snakes.

Some issues

- Which fears do you share?

- Some fears seem to be based on real threats, but others do not. Which fears do you think are not sensible?

- Why do you think there's a difference in phobias between genders and age?

- How can people learn to overcome their fears?

Source: YouGov
http://yougov.co.uk

Bullying

The MYTHS and the FACTS

MYTH: *Bullying is a normal part of growing up*

FACT: Bullying is NOT a normal part of growing up and it's NOT 'character building'

Adults do not expect to be hit, tripped or called names and threatened when they go to work. You have this same right to be free from bullying and to feel safe wherever you are. Bullying can make you feel depressed or lonely, it can affect your school work and make you dread going to school - this is not normal, you shouldn't have to feel like this.

MYTH: *Bullying is only physical*

FACT: Physical acts such as hitting, kicking and pushing are bullying, but bullying can take many different forms

These include:

- Being ignored, left out or having rumours spread about you;

- Having belongings stolen or damaged;

- Being called names, teased, put down or threatened;

- Cyberbullying;

- Receiving abusive text messages or emails;

- Being targeted for who you are or who you are perceived to be .

MYTH: *Only weak people are bullied*

FACT: Bullying is about how someone is viewed by other people

People may be seen as weak because they do not play a particular sport, they are shy, or they are the new person at a school. This does not mean that a person is weak. People who bully often pick on people that they feel they may have power over.

MYTH: *People bring bullying on themselves because of their behaviour*

FACT: No-one deserves to be bullied and no-one makes someone bully them

You have the right to be yourself, to wear what you want, to form your own opinions and be who you want to be. Life would be dull if everyone was the same. Differences make life interesting and they should be respected.

MYTH: Bullying only takes place at school - teachers should deal with it

FACT: Bullying can take place anywhere, both inside and outside of the school gates

This can include at football practice, the Girl Guides, the Scouts, the local youth club, in parks and on public transport. Yes teachers should and can deal with it but so should other adults - your parents, youth leaders, bus drivers, local police and even you - everyone has a role to play in tackling bullying behaviour.

MYTH: Telling will only make it worse - it's grassing and adults will just over-react

FACT: There is a difference between telling on someone to get them into trouble and telling on someone to help other people

If you or someone you know is being bullied, the best way to make it stop is to let an adult know what is happening. Pick an adult that you know and trust, and if you are worried about them over-reacting explain these fears to them. The last thing that any adult will want to do is make the situation and bullying worse, so be open and honest about what you would like to happen.

MYTH: There's nothing I can do to stop someone else being bullied

FACT: You can play an important role in stopping bullying

Refuse to join in with any bullying behaviour - but remember that by doing nothing people might think that you agree with the bullying. So, keep safe but do something. Tell a trusted adult about the behaviour. Get involved with any anti-bullying schemes you know of, such as buddy schemes, peer counselling or helping raise awareness of bullying through poster campaigns and school assemblies.

Although bullying behaviour can be different, each 'type' of bullying is just as hurtful and upsetting as the next.

You have the right NOT to be bullied.

Some issues

- Which myths about bullying have you heard before?

- Is the advice given here likely to work?

- Should someone who is bullied just stand up for themselves?

- What can be done to tackle bullying?

- Why don't some people accept that *"Differences make life interesting and they should be respected"*?

Source: respectme - Scotland's Anti-Bullying Service
www.respectme.org.uk

Reporting bullying

Bullying has always been a top concern for young people who contact ChildLine

During 2012/13, bullying was mentioned in *44,766* counselling sessions - this was an *8% increase* on the previous year.
30,387 of the young people mentioned it as their main concern.

Online bullying

There was an *87% increase* in counselling about online bullying.

4,500 young people contacted ChildLine for support and advice on how to deal with being bullied via social networking sites, chat rooms, online gaming sites, or via their mobile phone.

How old?

Online bullying affects a slightly older age group compared with other types of bullying.

Age group	% of all contact about bullying	% of all contact about ONLINE bullying
12-18 year	72%	84%
11 and under	28%	16%

66% of young people said they were being bullied about their physical appearance or for being different. This left them feeling ashamed and too embarrassed to tell anyone about it.

Photo posed by models

> "I used to be proud of my roots until I started getting bullied at school because I look different to everyone else in my year. ... I used to be confident but now I'm shy. My friends tell me to ignore it but it's really difficult not to care."
>
> *Girl aged 13*

Photo posed by model

> "My school is rubbish - I don't like going. I'm being bullied by a group of boys and I don't know why. I've tried my best to avoid them but they always come and find me to push and kick me around. My teacher hasn't done anything to help, they've just told me to try and avoid them."
>
> *Boy aged 11*

School bullying

ChildLine found that most bullying happened in school: **19,795** young people said this.

11% told ChildLine that they had felt too scared to tell anyone - they believed that speaking out would make things worse.

Nearly **8,500** young people said they'd actively sought help from a teacher at school - unfortunately in many cases the same children said they had been left feeling that little or nothing had been done to stop the bullying.

Some issues

- Why is school the worst place for bullying?

- How could teachers be more effective in dealing with bullying?

- Is bullying happening more often or are people more likely to report it?

- How could you help someone who is being bullied?

Source: ChildLine - What's affecting children in 2013 - Can I tell you something? Report www.childline.org.uk

Impact of cyberbullying

On a scale of 1 to 10, how would you rate the impact that cyberbullying had on areas of your life?
(1 means no impact and 10 means extreme impact)

Self esteem	7.65
Social life	6.34
Optimism	5.98
Studies	4.98
Home life	4.77
Future career	3.73

Photo: posed by model

"Every chance people can get they put me down and make me feel like a freak just because I'm gay. I feel more comfortable on websites where my sexual preference is widely accepted..."

Male, 17

Useful organisations

Cyberbullying is no less serious than offline bullying. It is important to talk about what you have been through with trusted adults, friends or health professionals.

ChildLine: **0800 1111**
www.childline.org.uk

NSPCC helpline: **0808 800 5000**
www.nspcc.org.uk/cyberbullying

www.anti-bullyingalliance.org.uk

www.bullying.co.uk

Guide to cyberbullying for teens:
www.ditchthelabel.org/dealing-with-cyberbullying

Some issues

- Why is cyberbullying so widespread?

- Do the sites have some responsibility to prevent or monitor this?

- Should the police or other services intervene with online bullying? Who else can help?

- How can you keep yourself safe online?

Source: © Ditch the Label Annual Cyberbullying Survey 2013; NSPCC www.ditchthelabel.org www.nspcc.org.uk

Education

World class education

The UK has a good reputation for its Higher Education

18-34 year olds from Brazil, China, Germany, India and US were asked*
How much do you agree that the UK has world-leading universities and academic research?
(Base: 5,029)

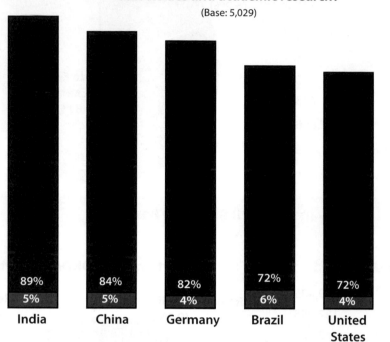

■ Agree

■ Disagree

The remainder neither
agreed nor disagreed

Country	Agree	Disagree
India	89%	5%
China	84%	5%
Germany	82%	4%
Brazil	72%	6%
United States	72%	4%

*The British Council selected countries with whom the UK wished to connect for business, tourism etc and asked young, educated people a series of questions about what makes a country attractive.

18-34 year olds from Brazil, China, Germany, India and UK and the US were asked:

Which three countries from this list do you find the most attractive as a country in which to study?

Australia, Brazil, Canada, China, France, Germany, India, Italy, Japan, Mexico, Russia, South Korea, Spain, United Kingdom, United States

The most attractive top 5 countries chosen were:

US	**67%**
UK	**42%**
Australia	**39%**
Canada	**33%**
France	**27%**

Some issues

- How do you think the people questioned formed their views on the education system in the UK?

- Should the UK be making efforts to attract students from other countries?

- What are the incentives for foreign students to study in the UK?

- Would you consider studying abroad?

Base: 6,051 18-34 year olds from Brazil, China, Germany, India, US, GB

Source: Research by Ipsos MORI and In2Impact for the British Council - As Others See Us www.britishcouncil.org

---

Environment

Climate or coal?

Coal-fired power plants are the single biggest global source of greenhouse gases

CO2

Carbon Dioxide, CO2, is a natural and essential part of the cycle of life on Earth.

However, when power stations burn fossil fuels such as coal to produce electricity they release waste gases, including extra amounts of CO2. These gases slow down the natural loss of heat from the Earth's atmosphere. This changes the climate, causing the Earth to warm up more than is normal.

We refer to this as the greenhouse effect.

Top 10 CO2 polluting power plants in Europe, 2013

Country	Power plant	Electricity generated (Megawatts)	CO2 emissions (metric tonnes per annum)
Poland	Bełchatów	5,298	37.18
Germany	Neurath	4,168	33.28
Germany	Niederaussem	3,680	29.58
Germany	Jänschwalde	2,790	25.40
Germany	Boxberg	2,427	21.89
United Kingdom	Drax	3,300	20.32
Germany	Weisweiler	1,798	18.66
Greece	Agios Dimitrios	1,587	13.11
Italy	Brindisi Sud	2,640	11.81
Germany	Lippendorf	1,750	11.73

Europe's "Dirty Thirty"

Both **Germany** and the **UK** rely heavily on coal for their electricity and both have **9** coal-fired power plants in the **top 30** polluters in Europe.

Poland has **4**, **Italy** has **2**, **Greece** has **2**, **Netherlands** has **1**, **Estonia** has **1**, **Portugal** has **1**, **Spain** has **1**.

Emissions in the EU

Power plants that use coal make up just **40%** of world energy production, but they produce **more than 70%** of emissions which are responsible for climate change.

The EU is committed to reducing greenhouse gas emissions - but economic pressures may take priority.

There has been an overall decrease in total EU greenhouse gas emissions but CO2 emissions from coal fired power plants have risen recently.

The lower price of coal compared to gas means that many of the EU's coal-fired plants are being used more than gas power plants.

This is one of the reasons for a rise in emissions as coal releases twice as much CO2 as gas does.

The use of renewable energy, such as solar panels and onshore wind turbines, has helped to cut CO2 emissions but the increase in electricity generated from coal between 2009 and 2012 has partially offset this.

Drax power station in the UK which ranks 6th in Europe's "Dirty Thirty"

Pollution from burning coal has a major impact on human health as well as the environment

Burning coal releases nitrogen oxides, sulphur dioxide, dust and heavy metals such as mercury and arsenic.

These pollutants are major causes of acid rain and smog and there are clear links to air pollution and the biggest chronic diseases in Europe such as heart disease, asthma and lung cancer.

Half of the health damage from all the major industrial activities of the EU, is caused by just **2%** of all installations. The coal power plants listed in the "Dirty 30" are all among these top **2%**.

They alone are responsible for **20%** of all power sector health costs, or **14%** of total industrial sector health costs in the EU.

The future for coal

In the UK, **31%** of electricity currently comes from coal-burning power stations. However, **33%** of these power stations are expected to close by 2016 so that they meet EU air quality legislation.

This means that we will become less reliant on coal as a source of energy and will need to look at alternative energy sources.

A developing technology called Carbon Capture and Storage (CCS) which removes CO_2 from power station emissions and stores it underground might help the UK to cut its emissions and meet its international climate change targets.

Some issues

- We are using more and more electricity yet we want a clean and healthy environment. Can we really achieve both these aims?

- What can we do to reduce the amount of electricity we use?

- Should there be more restrictions regarding air pollution or fewer?

- From the table, is it possible to see a relationship between the electricity generated and the amount of CO_2 emitted?

Source: WWF:
awsassets.panda.org/downloads/dirty_30_report_finale.pdf ,
Energy UK : www.energy-uk.org.uk/energy-industry/coal-generation.html

Have you done any of the following for environmental reasons in the past month?
(more than one answer could be given)

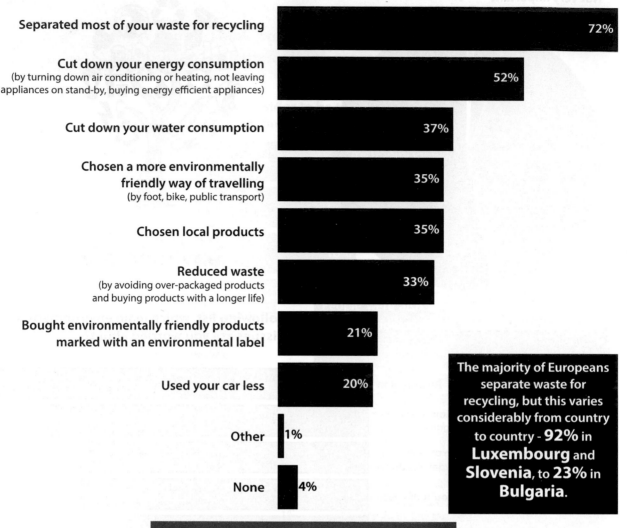

Separated most of your waste for recycling — **72%**

Cut down your energy consumption
(by turning down air conditioning or heating, not leaving appliances on stand-by, buying energy efficient appliances) — **52%**

Cut down your water consumption — **37%**

Chosen a more environmentally friendly way of travelling
(by foot, bike, public transport) — **35%**

Chosen local products — **35%**

Reduced waste
(by avoiding over-packaged products and buying products with a longer life) — **33%**

Bought environmentally friendly products marked with an environmental label — **21%**

Used your car less — **20%**

Other — **1%**

None — **4%**

The majority of Europeans separate waste for recycling, but this varies considerably from country to country - **92%** in **Luxembourg** and **Slovenia**, to **23%** in **Bulgaria**.

75% of Europeans said they are willing to pay a little more for environmentally friendly products.

RE USE DUCE CYCLE

Some issues

- If you were asked the same question about the most important problems facing the world, what would your answer be, and why?

- Which environmental issue worries you most?

- Can small changes by individuals really make a difference to the environment?

- What should governments do to tackle environmental issues?

- Are there any environmental issues in your area you would consider taking action about?

Base: Two EU28 surveys both with over 28,000 respondents

*Source: European Commission Eurobarometer surveys: Climate Change and Attitudes of European citizens towards the environment
http://ec.europa.eu*

Family & relationships

Separation & divorce

Young people are struggling to cope with family problems

35,154 young people gave family relationship problems as their main reason for contacting ChildLine during 2012/13.

The biggest increase in the reasons given for contacting ChildLine was parents' divorce and separation - a **122%** increase.

Age breakdown of young people who were counselled about their parents' divorce and separation

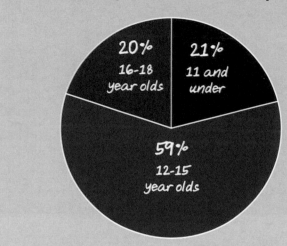

- 20% 16-18 year olds
- 21% 11 and under
- 59% 12-15 year olds

Separation peaks in the new year

Couples and families spend much more time together during the Christmas and New Year holidays which can highlight relationship problems.

Relate, which offers relationship support to couples, families and young people, received a **53%** increase in calls and an **86%** increase in appointments booked on the first Monday of January 2014 compared to the first Monday of the previous month.

"I can't do anything right. I found out about something my mum was doing and I told my dad about it. I feel like I wrecked the family because they split up after this. "

Girl aged 15

" My mum and dad are going through a divorce at the moment. Dad's already left and I haven't seen him for a while, which makes me feel sad. "

Boy aged 11

What parents thought about the impact on children of their separation and divorce

Base: Relate surveyed 1,537 adults in 2013

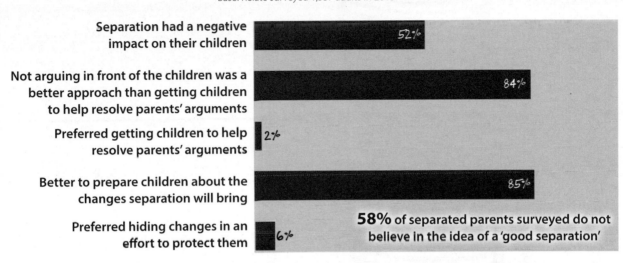

Separation had a negative impact on their children — 52%

Not arguing in front of the children was a better approach than getting children to help resolve parents' arguments — 84%

Preferred getting children to help resolve parents' arguments — 2%

Better to prepare children about the changes separation will bring — 85%

Preferred hiding changes in an effort to protect them — 6%

58% of separated parents surveyed do not believe in the idea of a 'good separation'

Separation and divorce aren't one-off events which start and end when one parent leaves home - **40%** said it took less than a year, **43%** said between 1 and 4 years and **10%** said it took 5 years or more.

Before, during and after separation kids often pick up more than we realise... having knock-on effects including problems at school, alcohol misuse and mental health and wellbeing issues.

Ruth Sutherland
Chief Executive of Relate

ChildLine: 0800 1111

Relate: 0300 100 1234

Some issues

- Should parents be open about problems?

- Who should decide what is best for the children when parents split up?

- How can children cope with their parents separating?

- What help should be available during divorce and to prevent divorce?

See also Self-harm, p186

Sources: Relate www.relate.org.uk
Can I tell you something? Childline Review 2012/13
www.childline.org.uk

Finance

Students & money

What financial issues do students face?

How concerned are students about money?

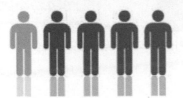

4 in 5
constantly
worry about
MONEY

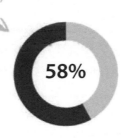

46% Affects **STUDIES**

58% Affects **DIET**

What do students spend their money on?

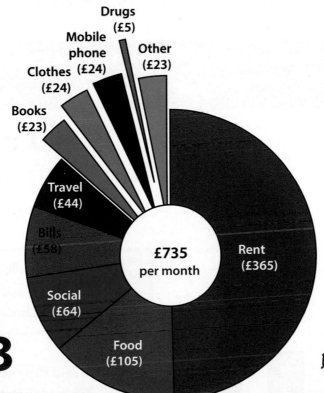

Drugs (£5)
Mobile phone (£24)
Clothes (£24)
Other (£23)
Books (£23)
Travel (£44)
Bills (£58)
Social (£64)
Food (£105)
Rent (£365)

£735 per month

"We should be given finance lessons when coming to uni, most students have never had to budget before"

1 in 3
HAVE NEVER
BUDGETED

Biggest changes over 2013

Rent has *increased* by £7 and spending on *food* has *decreased* by £38

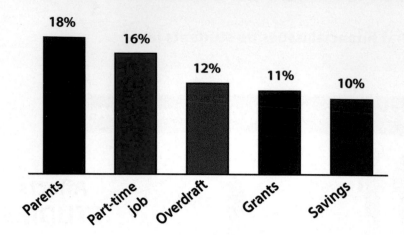

Top 5 sources of money for students

- Parents 18%
- Part-time job 16%
- Overdraft 12%
- Grants 11%
- Savings 10%

"Having to work is having an impact on my studies and my relationship"

"I'd rather accept more debt and not be reliant on my parents!"

"I rely on my parents for everything and they can't really afford to keep giving me money every week just so I can eat"

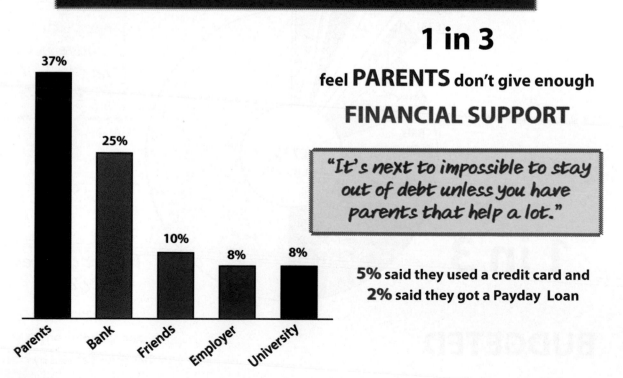

Where do students get money in an emergency? Top five methods

- Parents 37%
- Bank 25%
- Friends 10%
- Employer 8%
- University 8%

1 in 3

feel **PARENTS** don't give enough **FINANCIAL SUPPORT**

"It's next to impossible to stay out of debt unless you have parents that help a lot."

5% said they used a credit card and **2%** said they got a Payday Loan

How do students feel about their student loans?

50%

worry about repaying
student loan

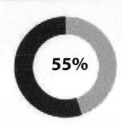

55%

don't understand loan
repayment conditions

> "Some students I know have dropped out
> of their course due to money worries"

80% worry about **life after uni**

> "It's not difficult to live
> within your means... some
> people just don't know what
> their means are."

> "Before university I had nearly £5,000 in life savings. I will have
> used all of it funding my university life before I graduate."

Is university worth it?

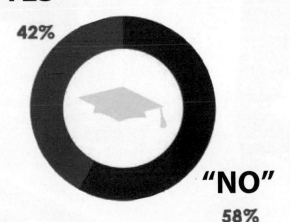

"YES"

42%

"NO"

58%

Some issues

- Are you surprised that the majority of students think that university is not worth it?

- Do you think that opinion is based just on finance or are there other factors?

- Do you think what students say they spend money on is accurate?

- Should students get more support from the government to help them through university?

Base: 2,820 students

Source: National Student Money Survey - Save the Student!
www.savethestudent.org

Social life

A fear of appearing less than generous encourages people to overspend when they're socialising

The Money Advice Service questioned 3,000 UK adults about their spending habits. **58%** worried that they would appear 'tight' in front of others and **32%** admitted that this contributed to their overspending when out.

Debt

48% of those questioned admitted to falling into debt as a result of their social lives.

The annual 'social debt' among this group was **£1,260** with **56%** of all UK adults saying they usually spent more than they planned to on social occasions.

Control

A lack of self-control is a key reason for 'social debt' with **36%** simply getting carried away and overspending.

However, when people DID try to control their spending, **35%** felt positive about being sensible. **33%** felt great about not wasting money and **20%** felt proud of themselves.

Pressure to spend

Social pressures added to this, with an average of **£341** spent per year, purely to avoid looking mean.

As a result, **20%** had to cut back on food due to their social spending and **9%** had not been able to pay utility bills.

Pub pressure

67% of all the adults questioned bought rounds of drinks at the pub and expected to spend more than they received back.

35% thought people who DIDN'T buy rounds of drinks were mean while **34%** felt they were being rude.

Photo: ChameleonsEye/Shutterstock.com

Eating out

When out for a meal **32%** of adults feel they lost out by paying for more than they had eaten - only **26%** said they split the bill based on what each person had eaten when out with friends, with **59%** saying that they felt uncomfortable suggesting this.

No money? No problem!

Not being able to say 'no' to a night out or social occasion also encourages social debt.

25% said they had been for meals out that they can't afford and **17%** had been on a holiday or break in the last year which they didn't have the money for.

Helpful tips from Money Advice Service

- Be honest if you can't afford the trip or holiday that friends want you to go on. Real friends won't pressure you to do something you can't really afford.

- Use cash while out instead of a card and set a budget to stick to.

- Alcohol impairs judgement - what seems like a good idea at the time might be something you'll regret the following morning.

- Having fun doesn't mean having to spend a lot of money. Search online for free things to do in your area, there are plenty of activities that you can do without spending anything.

Jenni Trent Hughes, Social Psychology Expert

Some issues

- What other occasions and events push you into spending too much?

- Are there any fair ways to even out spending when you go out with a group of friends?

- Why might people feel uncomfortable about saying they can't afford something?

- Should people just save for holidays and nights out instead of treating themselves to things they can't afford?

- Is this sort of spending a problem?

Source: Money Advice Service
www.moneyadviceservice.org.uk

Family spending

What do we spend our money on?

Average weekly household spend, UK

Figures do not add up to total due to rounding. Latest available figures 2012

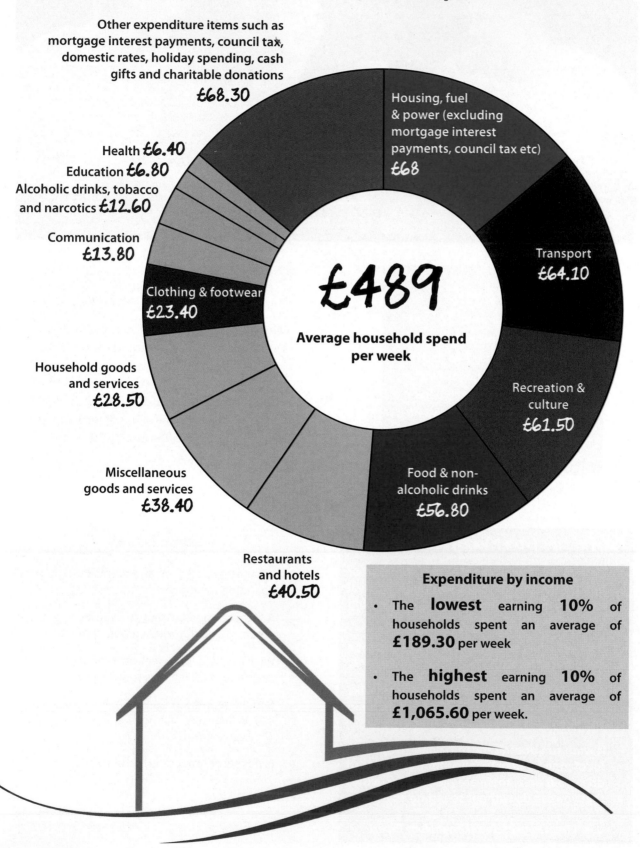

Other expenditure items such as mortgage interest payments, council tax, domestic rates, holiday spending, cash gifts and charitable donations **£68.30**

Health **£6.40**

Education **£6.80**

Alcoholic drinks, tobacco and narcotics **£12.60**

Communication **£13.80**

Clothing & footwear **£23.40**

Household goods and services **£28.50**

Miscellaneous goods and services **£38.40**

Restaurants and hotels **£40.50**

Housing, fuel & power (excluding mortgage interest payments, council tax etc) **£68**

Transport **£64.10**

Recreation & culture **£61.50**

Food & non-alcoholic drinks **£56.80**

£489

Average household spend per week

Expenditure by income

- The **lowest** earning **10%** of households spent an average of **£189.30** per week

- The **highest** earning **10%** of households spent an average of **£1,065.60** per week.

Housing, fuel & power

Electricity, gas and other fuels made up **£23.20** of the **£68** spent and the amount spent on rent came to **£29.30** a week (after removing housing benefit and related allowances).

Transport

Spending on petrol - **£16.40**, combined with diesel - **£8.20**, accounted for almost **40%** of the transport costs. **£10.50** was spent on rail, tube and bus fares.

Recreation & culture

This category includes spending on TVs, computers, newspapers, books and leisure activities. **£16.80** per week was spent on package holidays abroad, compared with **£1.50** a week on package holidays in the UK.

Food & non-alcoholic drinks

£15.00 of the total spent was on meat and fish, **£4.20** on fresh vegetables, and **£3.20** on fresh fruit.

Clothing & footwear

Expenditure on clothing has increased over time, despite the overall drop in the price of clothing. Households spent on average **£8.10** on women's outer garments and **£5.00** on men's outer garments per week.

Expenditure by Region

- Residents of London spent the most over the years 2010-12 combined, with a household average of **£571.60** per week; those in the North East spent the least at **£408.70** per week.

- London, the South East, the East and the South West showed expenditure **higher than the UK average.**

- The North East, Wales and Yorkshire & The Humber had the **lowest average spending**.

- London was the highest spending region on **housing, fuel and power - £97.50** per week over the 2010-2012 period.

- The South East was the highest spending region on **transport - £80.20** per week.

- Spending in rural areas is higher overall than in urban areas.

Some issues

- Are you surprised by the amount spent in any of the categories?

- How do you feel about the difference between the lowest and highest earning households?

- What could explain the differences between the regions?

- What can be done to help families spend less?

Source: Office for National Statistics
Crown copyright © December 2013 **www.ons.gov.uk**

Spending power

The items used to calculate inflation have changed over time

The Consumer Price Index

Inflation is an increase in the general price of goods and services over a period of time. As inflation goes up your spending power goes down as each pound buys a smaller amount.

The Consumer Price Index (CPI) is the government's way of showing the effect of inflation on your purchasing power.

It is a very detailed measurement but an easy way of thinking about this is to imagine a very large shopping basket containing those goods and services usually bought by households.

Every year, over 700 items are included in the basket. Some items have to be changed to keep spending patterns up to date

This means that a look back at the CPI shows us changes in the way we spend our money and the way we live.

Whilst some items change each year, many household goods and services have been in the basket for a very long time: milk, bread and tea for example, have been there since 1947 whilst petrol and diesel have been there since 1987.

Developments in technology every year and changing trends influence what is added to and removed from the basket. The overall size of the basket is limited each year so a number of items have to be removed to make space for the new additions.

ITEMS THAT HAVE ENTERED THE BASKET   **ITEMS THAT HAVE LEFT THE BASKET**

The items shown in the diagrams are just a selection of items that have entered and left the shopping basket, not the entire list of items

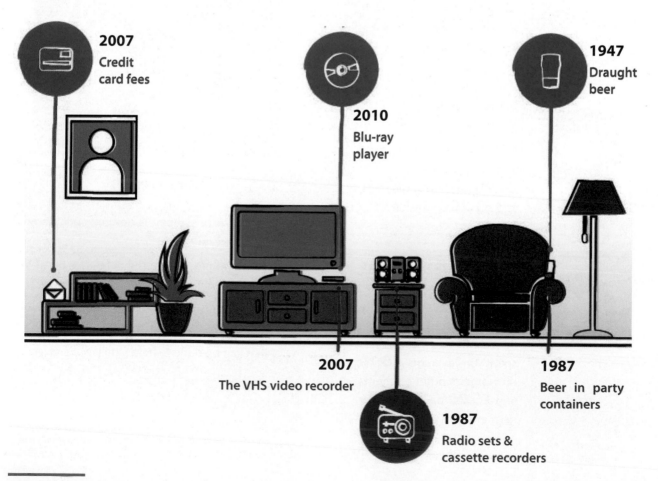

2007
Credit card fees

2010
Blu-ray player

1947
Draught beer

2007
The VHS video recorder

1987
Radio sets & cassette recorders

1987
Beer in party containers

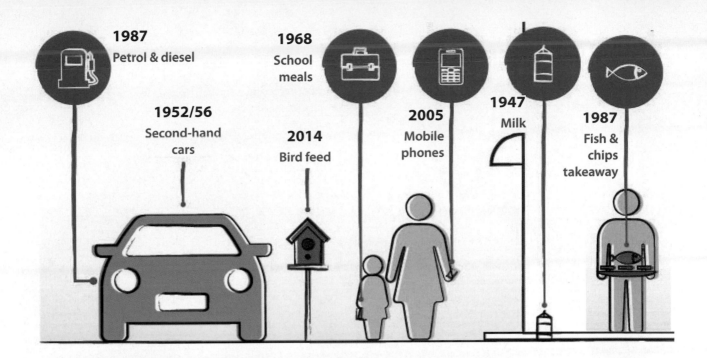

1987 Petrol & diesel

1968 School meals

1952/56 Second-hand cars

2014 Bird feed

2005 Mobile phones

1947 Milk

1987 Fish & chips takeaway

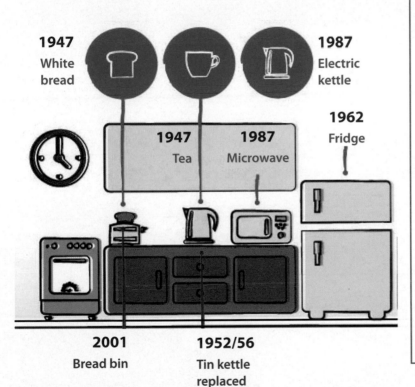

1947 White bread

1987 Electric kettle

1947 Tea

1987 Microwave

1962 Fridge

2001 Bread bin

1952/56 Tin kettle replaced

Added to basket 2014

Interchangeable lens digital cameras - as digital compact cameras become less popular because of mobile phone cameras.

Other items added include: **Programme streaming, Plant food, Men's clothing hire, Canvas fashion shoes**

Flavoured milk and fresh fruit snacking pots were added to the basket to diversify the milk and fresh fruit sections.

Honey was added to the sugar, jam, syrups, chocolate and confectionery group.

Fashion necklaces were added to cover the costume jewellery group.

Removed from basket 2014

The **DVD recorder** has been removed and DVD rental has been replaced by **DVD rental/video on demand subscription.**

Other items removed include: **wallpaper paste, hardwood flooring, gardeners' fees, after school club charges.**

In some cases a product is still represented in the basket, for example, **take-away coffee** has been removed but is still covered by take-away latte.

Some issues

- Why is it important to know about inflation?
- Can you understand why some articles are removed and others included?
- What do you predict will be included in the future?

Source: Consumer Price Inflation: The 2014 Basket of Goods and Services © Office for National Statistics 2014
www.ons.gov.uk

Gender

Facing the issues

Body image, self-esteem, relationships, everyday sexism – these are just some of the issues girls face on a daily basis

Girlguiding is the leading charity for girls and young women in the UK. Girlguiding's fifth Girls' Attitudes Survey provides a unique overview of the issues facing girls aged 7 to 21 in the UK today.

75% think sexism affects most areas of their lives (11 to 21)

60% of girls have had comments shouted at them about their appearance at school and **62%** have been shouted or whistled at in the street about their appearance.

80% think there is too much discussion about women's weight in the media and **71%** say they would like to lose weight.

87% think women are judged more for their looks than ability (11 to 21)

76% say girls are judged harshly for sexual behaviour seen as acceptable in boys (11 to 21)

53% of all girls think that too much responsibility is placed on girls for their sexual safety. **38%** of girls aged 16 to 21 feel that sex education has not prepared them well.

We want our children to grow up believing they can be anything they want to be. Clearly, for girls, sexism is still a major hurdle to that sense of freedom.
Laura Bates, founder of the Everyday Sexism Project

These pressures have an effect, and overall, girls are less positive this year than in previous years about the way they look and numbers who are not happy with their looks have increased.

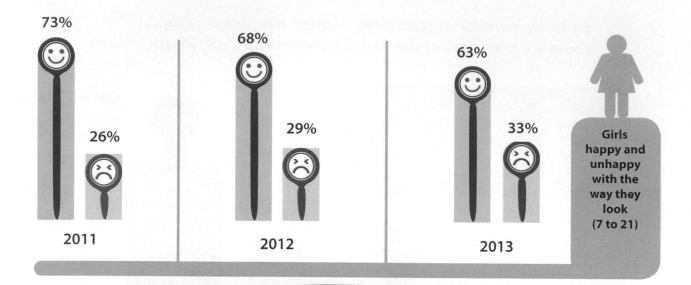

73%
26%
2011

68%
29%
2012

63%
33%
2013

Girls happy and unhappy with the way they look (7 to 21)

> It's far more difficult to be brave change-makers in the world, when the world repeatedly tells you that you're only here to look pretty! The media needs to be far more responsible and respectful in how it represents women.
> *Lucy-Anne Holmes, founder of the No More Page 3 campaign*

Role models:

This year's survey confirms that there is a serious 'role model deficit' for girls and young women and that this negatively affects some girls' aspirations.

66% of girls aged 11 to 21 think that there are not enough women in leadership positions in the UK. **54%** are to some extent put off by this, feeling that they have less chance of succeeding themselves. **29%** feel this quite strongly.

Resilience:

There is also strong resilience among girls and young women, with **46%** saying that the lack of women in leadership roles makes them feel more determined to succeed themselves. **29%** feel this quite strongly.

Despite all the challenges they face, girls and young women report that they want family and friends and education and a career in order to be happy.

What girls say they need in life to do well and be happy today (7 to 21)

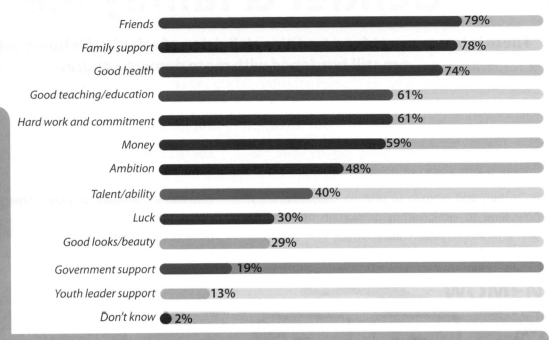

Friends	79%
Family support	78%
Good health	74%
Good teaching/education	61%
Hard work and commitment	61%
Money	59%
Ambition	48%
Talent/ability	40%
Luck	30%
Good looks/beauty	29%
Government support	19%
Youth leader support	13%
Don't know	2%

63%

say more female leaders would mean a better deal for women (11 to 21)

There are still three times as many men as women in Parliament...We're constantly being told that what matters is how much we weigh, or how pretty men think we are, instead of what we can achieve. It's a tough world, and we've got a lot of work to do, but there's a lot to be excited about.

My advice to any young woman is to go for it - stand up for what you believe in no matter what anyone tells you.
Caroline Lucas, MP for Brighton Pavilion

An equal future:

It is clear that today's generation of girls and young women are positive, resilient and ambitious, and have the potential to be a powerful force for change in society.

The report presents clear evidence that we are too often failing to provide safe and equal environments in which girls can flourish and grow up to reach their full potential.

Some issues

- What can be done to tackle sexism?

- Why is there more focus on girls' appearance than on boys'?

- Are single-sex institutions like girl-guiding important?

Source: Equality for Girls, Girls' Attitudes survey 2013
www.girlguiding.org.uk

Equality

The majority of people believe women SHOULD be equal to men, yet many women still don't believe they ARE

"I believe in equal opportunities for men and women – that women should be treated equally to men in all areas based on their competency not their gender"

All respondents: % who agree or disagree

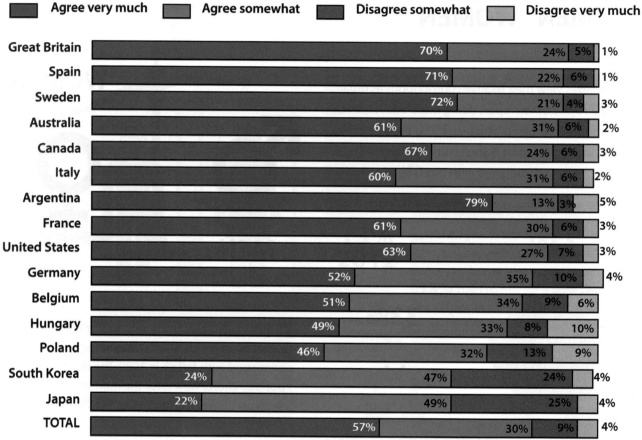

	Agree very much	Agree somewhat	Disagree somewhat	Disagree very much
Great Britain	70%	24%	5%	1%
Spain	71%	22%	6%	1%
Sweden	72%	21%	4%	3%
Australia	61%	31%	6%	2%
Canada	67%	24%	6%	3%
Italy	60%	31%	6%	2%
Argentina	79%	13%	3%	5%
France	61%	30%	6%	3%
United States	63%	27%	7%	3%
Germany	52%	35%	10%	4%
Belgium	51%	34%	9%	6%
Hungary	49%	33%	8%	10%
Poland	46%	32%	13%	9%
South Korea	24%	47%	24%	4%
Japan	22%	49%	25%	4%
TOTAL	57%	30%	9%	4%

Research was conducted between 4-18th February, 2014. An international sample of 12,047 people in 15 countries was interviewed, 6,188 were women.

NB Figures may not add to 100% due to rounding

"I have full equality with men and the freedom to reach my full dreams and aspirations"

Women: % who agree or disagree

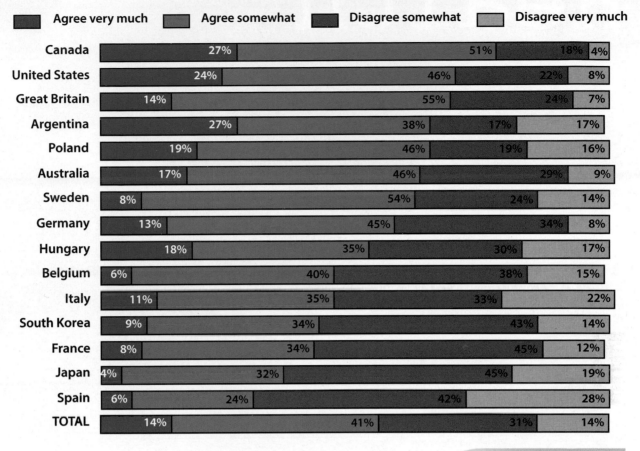

	Agree very much	Agree somewhat	Disagree somewhat	Disagree very much

Canada	27%	51%	18%	4%
United States	24%	46%	22%	8%
Great Britain	14%	55%	24%	7%
Argentina	27%	38%	17%	17%
Poland	19%	46%	19%	16%
Australia	17%	46%	29%	9%
Sweden	8%	54%	24%	14%
Germany	13%	45%	34%	8%
Hungary	18%	35%	30%	17%
Belgium	6%	40%	38%	15%
Italy	11%	35%	33%	22%
South Korea	9%	34%	43%	14%
France	8%	34%	45%	12%
Japan	4%	32%	45%	19%
Spain	6%	24%	42%	28%
TOTAL	14%	41%	31%	14%

Only **55%** of WOMEN think they have full equality with men yet the same research showed that an average of only **57%** of ALL respondents actively speak up to try to change things for women.

"I am scared to speak out and advocate the equal rights of women because of what might happen to me"

All respondents: % who agree

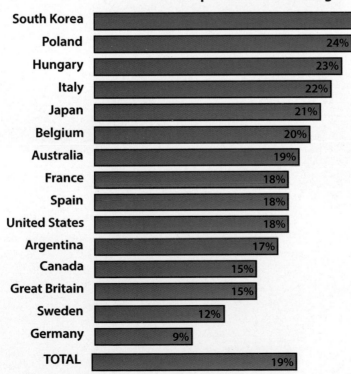

Country	%
South Korea	30%
Poland	24%
Hungary	23%
Italy	22%
Japan	21%
Belgium	20%
Australia	19%
France	18%
Spain	18%
United States	18%
Argentina	17%
Canada	15%
Great Britain	15%
Sweden	12%
Germany	9%
TOTAL	19%

Some issues

- Why do you think there are differences between how equal women feel in different countries?

- Why do you think some people feel scared to speak out for equality?

- What advantages are there for society as a whole in achieving gender equality?

Source: Feminism & gender equality in 15 developed countries, Ipsos MORI www.ipsos-mori.com

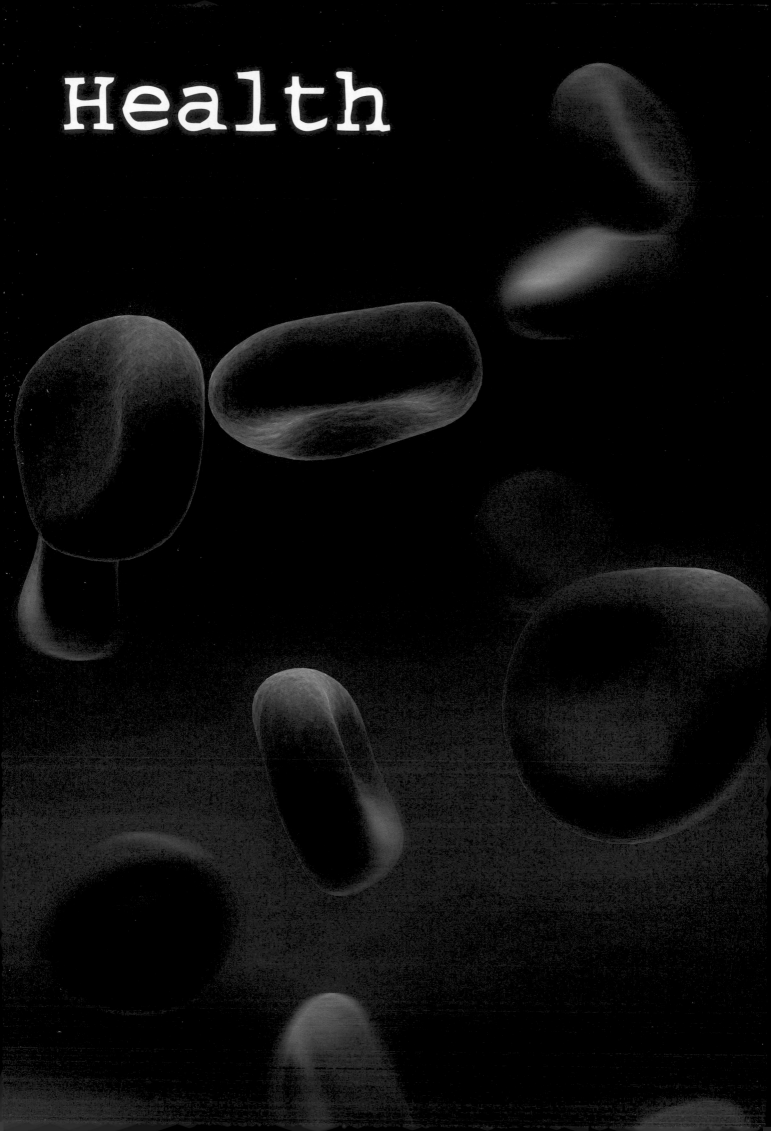

Health

Neglected health

UK's Mr and Mrs Average are not in average health, but are in fact tired, overweight, dehydrated and unfit!

Most people in the UK are not taking even the most basic measures to look after themselves.

Based on eight NHS health guidelines for men and women, Mrs Average generally has a healthier lifestyle than Mr Average.

Mrs Average sleeps more, eats more fresh fruit and veg, drinks and smokes less.

Mr Average takes more exercise, but he's also more likely to smoke and drink, which is likely to impact upon his general health.

Neither seem to be sticking to the guidelines!

Mr Average	Guidelines for men & women	Mrs Average
6.4 hrs of sleep	7-8 hours for both	6.5 hrs of sleep
Portions of fruit and veg per day: 3.3	5 a day for both	Portions of fruit and veg per day: 3.5
954ml of water a day	Women 1.6 litres, Men 2 litres	897ml of water a day
73 mins cardio[1] per wk	At least 150 mins cardio[1] per wk for both	69 mins cardio[1] per wk
1.4 muscle[2] workouts per wk	2 muscle[2] workouts per wk for both	1.1 muscle[2] workouts per wk
13.6 units of alcohol consumed per wk	Shouldn't regularly drink more than: 14 units per wk (women) 21 units per wk (men)	8.4 units of alcohol consumed per wk
3.8 cigarettes smoked per day	None	3.3 cigarettes smoked per day
Average BMI* 26.2	18.5 - 24.9 is a healthy BMI* range for both	Average BMI* 25.9

[1] eg: walking fast, water aerobics, hiking, riding a bike on level ground, pushing a lawnmower
[2] eg: lifting weights, push-ups, sit-ups, yoga, digging the garden

*Body Mass Index (BMI) is measured by comparing weight to height.

Past, present and future health

When looking at a timeline of 50 years ago through to 20 years in the future, it appears many people now feel we are currently at our most unhealthy.

People seem to believe that gradually the health of the UK is set to improve as we move into the future.

1964

Even though people had less access to information about health, fitness and nutrition 50 years ago, **72%** of people believed we were healthy compared to only **29%** who felt that we are healthy nowadays.

75% of women and **66%** of men believed that the UK was healthy 50 years ago compared to only **26%** of women and **32%** of men who believed the UK is healthy now.

1994-2004

70% of people believed that the UK was healthy back in the early 1990s

Between 1994 and 2004, people believed there was a decline in the UK's health - only **50%** thought that the UK was healthy 10 years ago.

2014

The view of the UK's health is currently bleak - half of the people surveyed thought the UK was not very healthy and **21%** thought the UK was not at all healthy.

People in Northern Ireland were the most positive though - **14%** thought the UK was very healthy.

2019

35% of people thought the UK would be healthy in 5 years' time.

Those aged 16-24 are one of the most optimistic age groups - **45%** said they thought the UK would be healthy in 2019.

London was the most optimistic region - **43%** thought that the UK would be healthy in 5 years' time.

2034

48% of people believed that the UK would be healthy in 20 years' time.

London was the most optimistic region again with **55%** agreeing, and the South West was the most negative with **62%** of people thinking the UK will be unhealthy.

Future of healthcare

66% of people now believe that the public should pay more in order to support the NHS.

34% believe this is necessary in order to continue to provide the basic healthcare expected in the UK, and a further **31%** believe this should happen because we have an ageing population to support.

22% believe that people should pay different amounts for health services, depending on how they actively manage their health.

But almost half of those surveyed thought the NHS shouldn't fund people who smoke, are obese, drink excessively or take recreational drugs.

Despite many people appearing to neglect their health:

47% see their GP 1-2 times per year

25% see their GP 3-5 times per year

41% of people will normally accept the advice/diagnosis of their GP, but will question them if they are unsure

35% will research their symptoms on the internet

13% will ensure that their doctor checks all their symptoms in great detail.

10% of people will ask to see a different doctor if they are not happy with the care provided.

Some issues

- What do the statistics from 'Mr and Mrs Average' tell us about the state of people's health in Britain?

- What do you think is involved in living a healthy lifestyle?

- Are there people who should not be treated on the NHS?

- Do you agree that we should all pay more to fund the health service.

Base: 4,123 UK adults

Source: Benenden Health National Health Report 2014
www.benenden.co.uk
NHS Choices
www.nhs.uk/livewell/fitness/Pages/Fitnesshome.aspx

Sickness absence

131 million days were lost to ill health in 2013, that's 4.4 days per worker

Top reasons for sickness absences

Minor illnesses such as coughs and colds were the most common reason given for sickness absence - these types of illnesses don't last long.

More days were lost to long-term illnesses such as back, neck and muscle pain than any other cause.

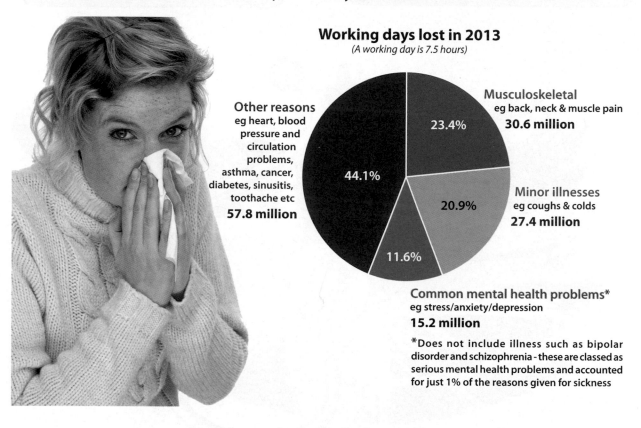

Working days lost in 2013
(A working day is 7.5 hours)

Other reasons
eg heart, blood pressure and circulation problems, asthma, cancer, diabetes, sinusitis, toothache etc
57.8 million

44.1%

23.4%

20.9%

11.6%

Musculoskeletal
eg back, neck & muscle pain
30.6 million

Minor illnesses
eg coughs & colds
27.4 million

Common mental health problems*
eg stress/anxiety/depression
15.2 million

*Does not include illness such as bipolar disorder and schizophrenia - these are classed as serious mental health problems and accounted for just 1% of the reasons given for sickness

Sickness absence rates, by gender
Percentage of working hours lost to sickness for **men** and women over time

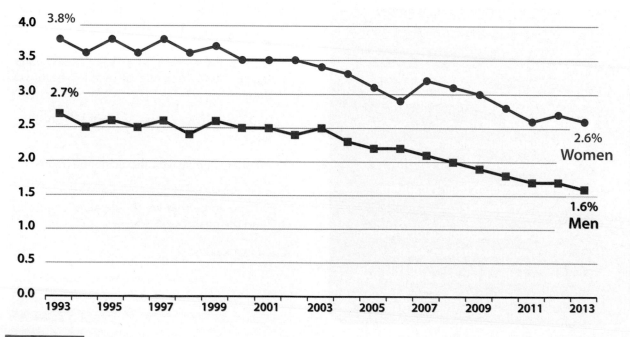

Age

As people get older they are more likely to develop health problems so sickness absence rates tend to increase with age.

2% of hours were lost to sickness for those workers **aged 35 to 49** and **2.8%** of hours lost to **50 to 64 year olds**.

Workers **aged 65 and over** lost a lower percentage of hours to sickness compared to **50 to 64 year olds**. This could be due to the fact that those with health problems are more likely to have left the working environment.

Percentage of working hours lost to sickness, by age group

■ **1993** ■ **2013**

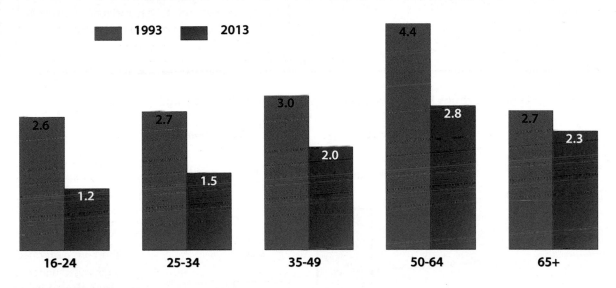

	1993	2013
16-24	2.6	1.2
25-34	2.7	1.5
35-49	3.0	2.0
50-64	4.4	2.8
65+	2.7	2.3

Absence by workplace size

Firms with more than 50 employees had higher percentages of working hours lost to sickness than smaller ones.

Firms with over 50 employees lost **2.3%** of working hours to sickness. Those with fewer than 25 members of staff lost **1.7%**.

In small workplaces, workers may not feel able to take time off due to work commitments, not having colleagues to cover their work and not wanting to let their team down.

Some issues

- Should you stay off work with a minor illness?

- Can you suggest why back, neck and muscle pain causes more days of absence?

- If you were an employer, would these figures influence you to choose workers from a particular age group?

- What can employers do to reduce the number of sick days?

Source: Sickness Absence in the Labour Market, February 2014
© Crown copyright 2014 **www.ons.gov.uk**

Abortions

Facts about the number, timing and frequency

Abortion means choosing to end a pregnancy.

In England, Wales and Scotland abortion is **legal** if you are **less than 24 weeks pregnant** and if two doctors agree that it is necessary for one of the following reasons:

- having a baby would upset your mental or physical health more than having an abortion. This means you need to explain to a doctor how you feel the pregnancy would affect your life;

- having the baby would harm the mental or physical health of any children you already have.

An abortion is also legal at any tIme in pregnancy if two doctors agree that:

- an abortion is necessary to save your life;

- an abortion would prevent serious permanent harm to your mental or physical health;

- there is a high risk that the baby would be born with a serious disability.

Unlike the rest of the UK, abortion is only allowed in very restricted circumstances in Northern Ireland. The only exceptions are to save a woman's life, or if there is a risk of permanent and serious damage to her mental or physical health, otherwise it is classed a criminal offence, which carries a life sentence.

Legal abortions for women resident in England & Wales, by age group, 2013

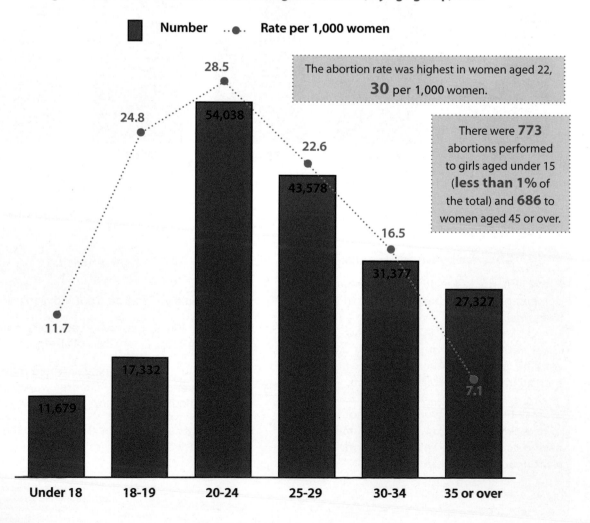

- ■ Number
- ⋯●⋯ Rate per 1,000 women

The abortion rate was highest in women aged 22, **30** per 1,000 women.

There were **773** abortions performed to girls aged under 15 (**less than 1%** of the total) and **686** to women aged 45 or over.

Age group	Number	Rate per 1,000 women
Under 18	11,679	11.7
18-19	17,332	24.8
20-24	54,038	28.5
25-29	43,578	22.6
30-34	31,377	16.5
35 or over	27,327	7.1

England & Wales, 2013
Resident women

The total number of abortions to women resident in England & Wales was **185,331** – a rate of **16.5** per 1,000 women aged 15-44.

Non-resident women

There were an additional **5,469** abortions performed for non-residents - the lowest in any year since 1969. **15%** were from **Northern Ireland** and **67%** of these women were from the **Irish Republic** where it is also currently illegal to have an abortion unless continuing the pregnancy would endanger the woman's life. **3%** were from Scotland and the remaining **15%** was made up of women from Europe and the rest of the world.

Scotland, 2013

The number and rate of abortions in Scotland has been decreasing since 2008. In 2013 the total number of abortions was **11,777** – a rate of **11.2** per 1,000 women aged 15-44 compared to **13,904** in 2008 - a rate of **13.3** per 1,000 women.

The fall in abortion rates was greatest in younger women down **33.7%** in those aged 16 to 19 and down **32.4%** in the under 16s.

The proportion of early terminations has been rising steadily in recent years with **69.2%** of all abortions performed at less than 9 weeks in 2013.

% of legal abortions, for women resident in England & Wales, by number of pregnancy weeks

■ 2003   ■ 2013

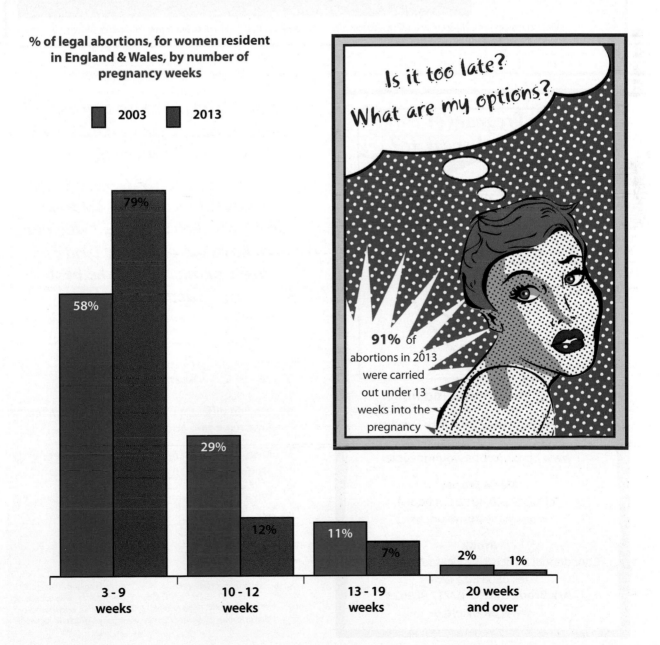

	2003	2013
3 - 9 weeks	58%	79%
10 - 12 weeks	29%	12%
13 - 19 weeks	11%	7%
20 weeks and over	2%	1%

Is it too late? What are my options?

91% of abortions in 2013 were carried out under 13 weeks into the pregnancy

Number of **previous** legal abortions, residents of England & Wales, 2013

Previous abortions

In 2013, **37%** of women in **England and Wales** and **30.7%** of women in **Scotland** undergoing abortions had previously had one or more previous abortions.

Number of previous abortions	Age group						Total
	Under 16	16 & 17	18 & 19	20 - 24	25 - 29	30 or over	
None	2,470	8,421	14,248	35,717	24,306	31,649	116,811
1	63	667	2,718	14,128	13,456	18,511	49,543
2	5	51	321	3,308	4,280	6,101	14,066
3	0	2	37	679	1,089	1,650	3,457
4	0	0	7	158	319	511	995
5	0	0	1	28	82	153	264
6	0	0	0	15	29	64	108
7	0	0	0	3	7	28	38
8 or more	0	0	0	2	10	37	49
Total	2,538	9,141	17,332	54,038	43,578	58,704	185,331

NB Percentages are subject to rounding and totals may not agree with the sum of the component figures shown

For useful advice and links:

British Pregnancy Advisory Services
Tel: 03457 30 40 30
www.bpas.org/bpasyoungpeople

Marie Stopes
Tel: 0845 300 80 90 (24 hours)
www.mariestopes.org.uk

Brook
Confidential advice & services for under-25s
Tel: 0808 802 1234
Ask Brook by text 07717 989023
www.brook.org.uk

> "I didn't think that I would get pregnant... I was only 15 and really worried.
>
> I went to a clinic where they listened to me and told me what my choices were. I decided to have an abortion and for me I think it was the best decision."
>
> *Hannah, age 19*

Some issues

- Why do different parts of the UK have different laws regarding abortion?

- Most abortions are carried out in the very early stages of pregnancy. Why is this important?

- What do you think of the current laws on abortion?

Source: Department of Health Abortion Statistics, England & Wales: 2013
© Crown copyright 2014 www.dh.gov.uk
NHS National Services Scotland www.nhsnss.org
British Pregnancy Advisory Service www.bpas.org/bpasyoungpeople

Causes of death

Medical advances in the treatment of many illnesses and diseases means that death rates are generally falling

During the 20th century, there have been steady decreases in death rates for the three main disease groups (**circulatory** eg heart disease and blood circulation problems, **cancer** and **respiratory** eg breathing problems). The reasons for this include:

- improvements in the treatment of these diseases

- preventative programmes eg NHS Breast screening
- campaigns to help improve people's health through better diet and lifestyle eg 'Change4life'
- 'Healthy Lives, Healthy People' strategy for England included a tobacco control plan and action to reduce obesity

Deaths per million population - the three main disease groups, England & Wales, 2012

Men

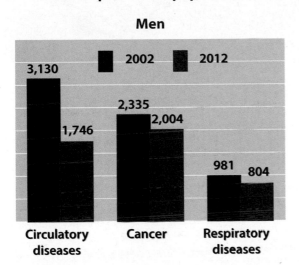

Women

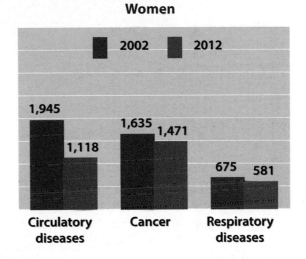

Total deaths registered, by age and gender

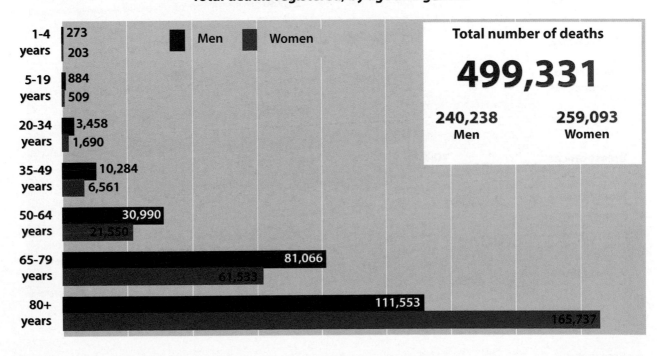

Total number of deaths

499,331

240,238
Men

259,093
Women

Leading causes of death in men

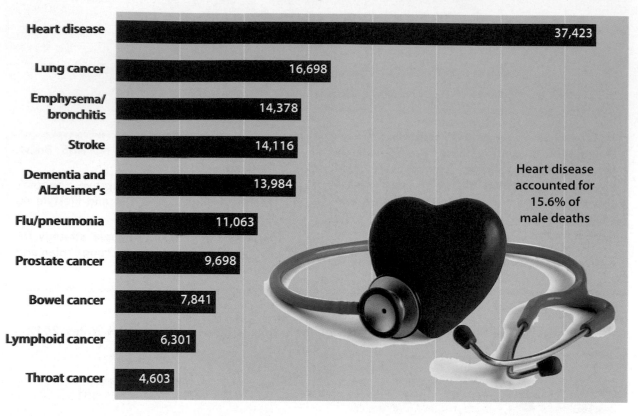

Cause	Deaths
Heart disease	37,423
Lung cancer	16,698
Emphysema/bronchitis	14,378
Stroke	14,116
Dementia and Alzheimer's	13,984
Flu/pneumonia	11,063
Prostate cancer	9,698
Bowel cancer	7,841
Lymphoid cancer	6,301
Throat cancer	4,603

Heart disease accounted for 15.6% of male deaths

Leading causes of death in women

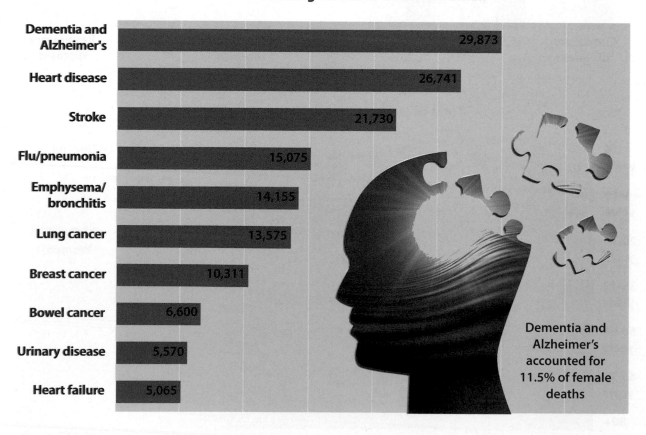

Cause	Deaths
Dementia and Alzheimer's	29,873
Heart disease	26,741
Stroke	21,730
Flu/pneumonia	15,075
Emphysema/bronchitis	14,155
Lung cancer	13,575
Breast cancer	10,311
Bowel cancer	6,600
Urinary disease	5,570
Heart failure	5,065

Dementia and Alzheimer's accounted for 11.5% of female deaths

Amongst younger age groups, the causes of death are less likely to be illness and more likely to be accident and suicide... but there are still differences between the male and female percentages

Leading causes of death, by gender and selected age groups

Male: 5-19 year olds
Total: 884 deaths

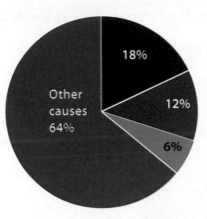

18%
12%
6%
Other causes 64%

- ● **1st** Land transport accidents
- ● **2nd** Suicide and injury/poisoning of undetermined intent
- ● **3rd** Malignant brain tumours, eg cancer

Female: 5-19 year olds
Total: 509 deaths

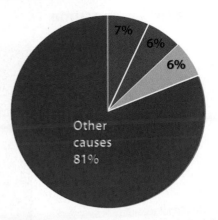

7%
6%
6%
Other causes 81%

- ● **1st** Birth defects such as Down's Syndrome
- ● **2nd** Malignant brain tumours, eg cancer
- ● **3rd** Malignant tumours affecting the blood and tissue eg leukaemia

Male: 20-34 year olds
Total: 3,458 deaths

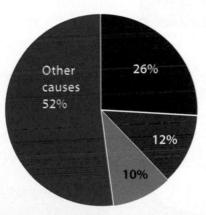

26%
12%
10%
Other causes 52%

- ● **1st** Suicide and injury/poisoning of undetermined intent
- ● **2nd** Accidental poisoning
- ● **3rd** Land transport accidents

Female: 20-34 year olds
Total: 1,690 deaths

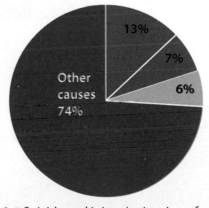

13%
7%
6%
Other causes 74%

- ● **1st** Suicide and injury/poisoning of undetermined intent
- ● **2nd** Accidental poisoning
- ● **3rd** Land transport accidents

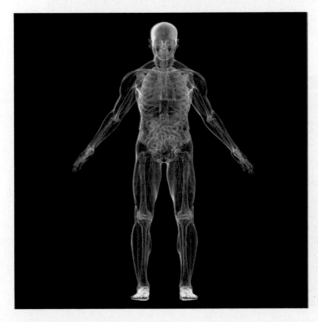

Some issues

- Can you suggest why the leading causes of death are different for men and women in general?

- Why would the main causes of death be different for the younger age groups than for older ones?

- What do the differences between male and female percentages in the 5-19 age group suggest to you?

Source: Deaths Registered in England and Wales, 2012, Office for National Statistics © 2013 www.ons.gov.uk

Salt

Although we are using less salt, we still consume too much

In the UK we consume **183,000,000 kg** of salt per year...this is equivalent to:

SALT 750g

240,000,000

standard 750g table salt containers

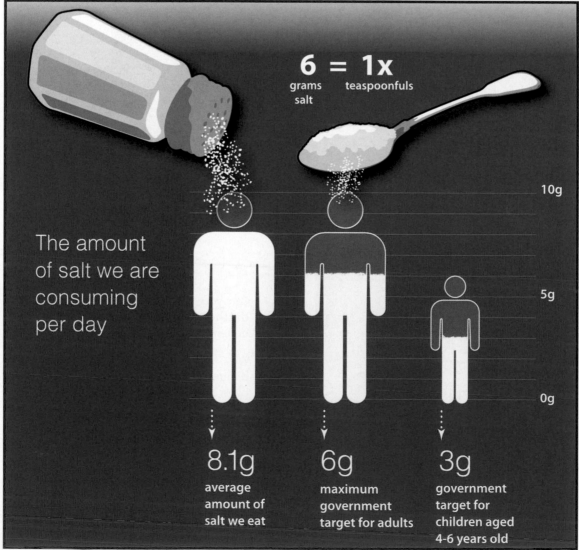

6 grams salt **= 1x** teaspoonfuls

The amount of salt we are consuming per day

10g

5g

0g

8.1g
average amount of salt we eat

6g
maximum government target for adults

3g
government target for children aged 4-6 years old

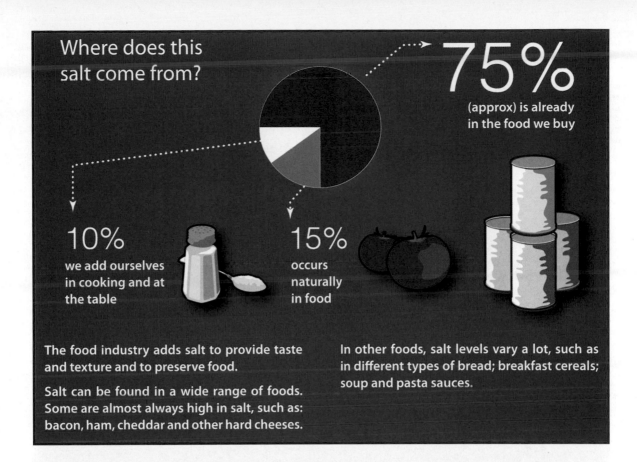

Where does this salt come from?

75% (approx) is already in the food we buy

10% we add ourselves in cooking and at the table

15% occurs naturally in food

The food industry adds salt to provide taste and texture and to preserve food.

Salt can be found in a wide range of foods. Some are almost always high in salt, such as: bacon, ham, cheddar and other hard cheeses.

In other foods, salt levels vary a lot, such as in different types of bread; breakfast cereals; soup and pasta sauces.

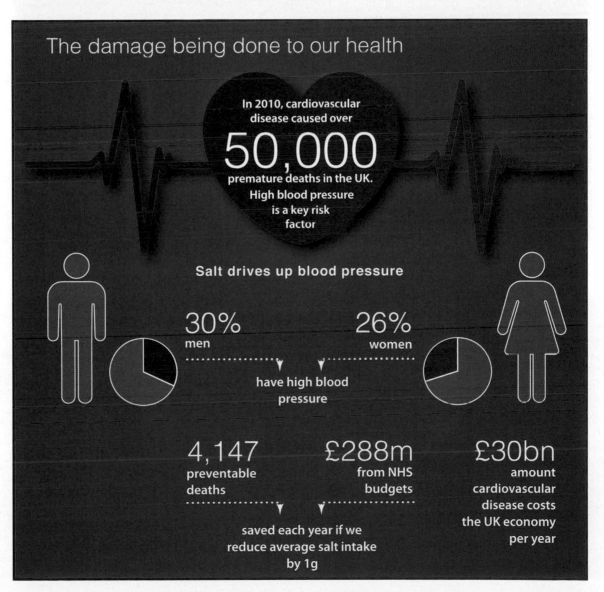

The damage being done to our health

In 2010, cardiovascular disease caused over **50,000** premature deaths in the UK. High blood pressure is a key risk factor

Salt drives up blood pressure

30% men

26% women

have high blood pressure

4,147 preventable deaths

£288m from NHS budgets

saved each year if we reduce average salt intake by 1g

£30bn amount cardiovascular disease costs the UK economy per year

How to cut down on salt: 3 top tips

1 When you buy food, check the label and choose the food that's lower in salt. Look at the figure for salt per 100g:

- HIGH is more than 1.5g of salt per 100g - may be colour-coded red.

- MEDIUM is between 0.3g and 1.5g of salt per 100g - may be colour-coded amber.

- LOW is 0.3g of salt or less per 100g - may be colour-coded green.

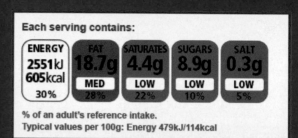

Each serving contains:

ENERGY 2551kJ 605kcal 30%	FAT 18.7g MED 28%	SATURATES 4.4g LOW 22%	SUGARS 8.9g LOW 10%	SALT 0.3g LOW 5%

% of an adult's reference intake.
Typical values per 100g: Energy 479kJ/114kcal

2 Eat foods which are high in salt less often, and eat them in smaller amounts. Use less ketchup, mustard, soy sauce and pickles as they are high in salt.

3 Cook with less salt:

- To season food, use black pepper, fresh herbs and spices instead.

- Make your own stock and gravy instead of using cubes or granules.

- Make sauces with fresh ingredients such as ripe tomatoes and garlic.

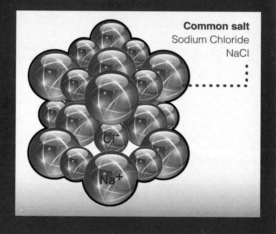

Common salt
Sodium Chloride
NaCl

Some issues

- Do food labels help you to make good choices?

- Why should the NHS be offering advice on food?

- Whose responsibility is it to make sure people make healthy choices?

- We know about the negative effects of salt, so why do we still use it?

*Source: NHS Choices **www.nhs.uk***

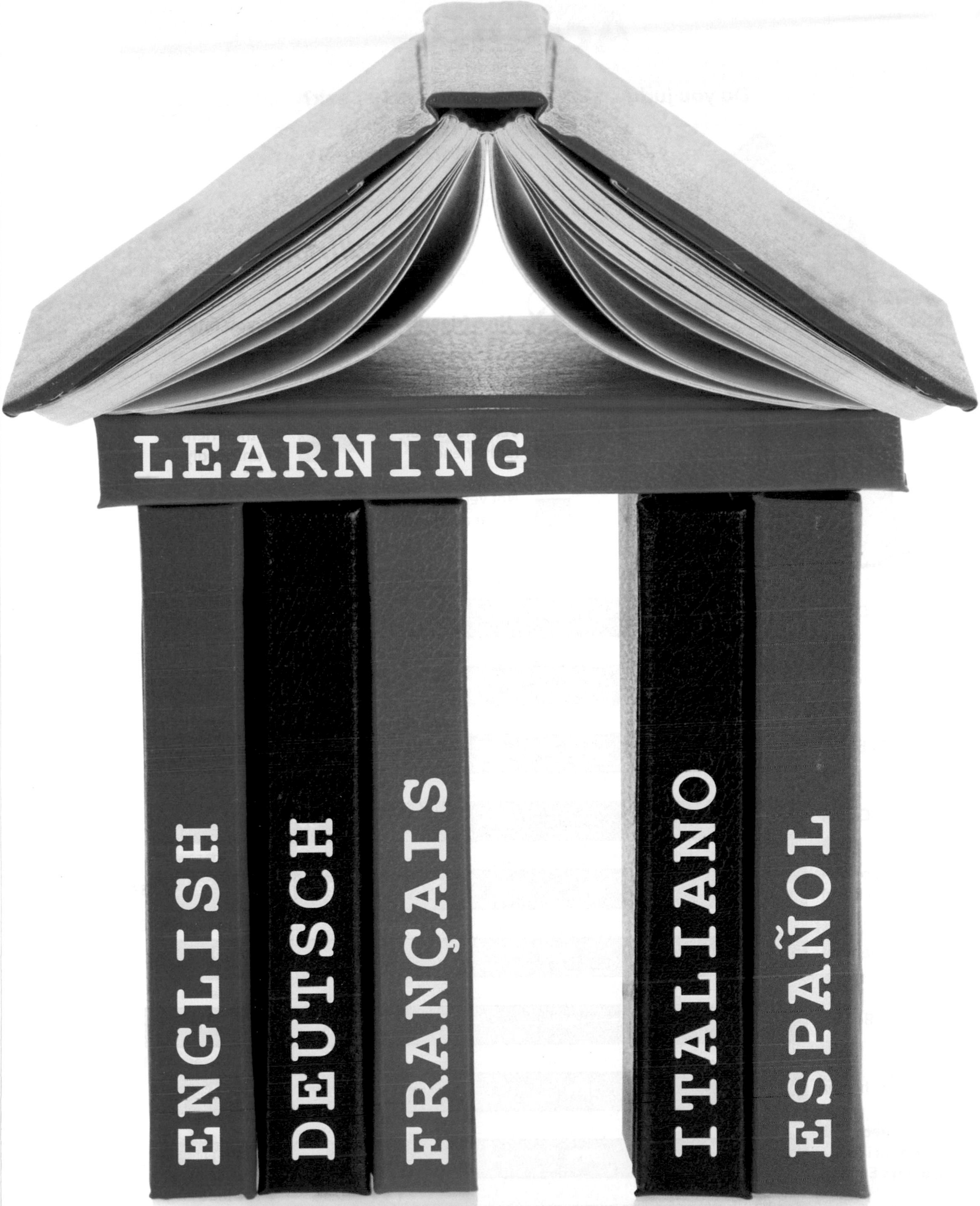

Language

Discrimination

Q Do you feel that you have ever **BEEN DISCRIMINATED AGAINST** because of your regional accent?

(Base: 2,014 GB adults)

12%	13%	14%	20%
In job interviews	**When being served in shops or restaurants**	**In the workplace**	**In a social situation**

Q Have you ever **PERSONALLY DISCRIMINATED AGAINST** someone because they had a particular regional accent?

(Base: 2,025 GB adults)

4%	6%	10%	14%
In job interviews	**In the workplace**	**In a social situation**	**On the telephone**

"We sound right scruffy like... not like you: posh. We won't be able to get proper jobs"

Child from Middlesbrough

"Every accent in Britain carries stories of its speaker...

I was shocked to discover that even the way we speak can make children feel like losers – before they really begin life's journey."

Penny Marshall is Social Affairs Editor for iTV News

Some issues

- Most people say they don't discriminate – how does that fit with the fact that they have strong views?

- What makes the Received Pronunciation accent trustworthy but not friendly?

- Why is the Devon accent preferred?

-

Source: ITV News Index surveys by ComRes, August/September 2013 **http://comres.co.uk**

Lost in translation

We think it's polite to speak the local language when travelling, but do not have enough time to learn it

Learning new languages

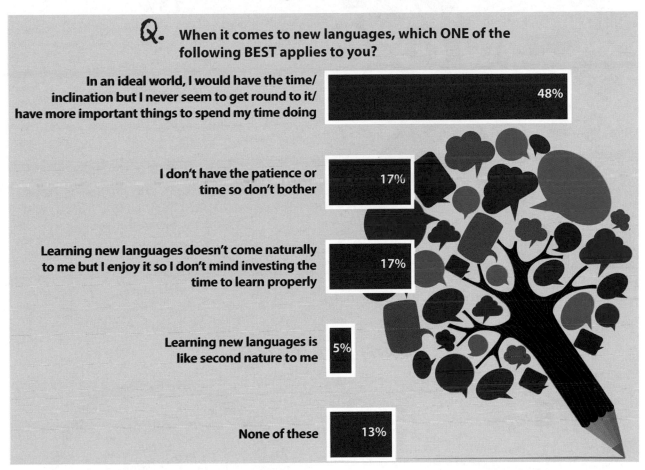

Q. When it comes to new languages, which ONE of the following BEST applies to you?

In an ideal world, I would have the time/inclination but I never seem to get round to it/have more important things to spend my time doing	48%
I don't have the patience or time so don't bother	17%
Learning new languages doesn't come naturally to me but I enjoy it so I don't mind investing the time to learn properly	17%
Learning new languages is like second nature to me	5%
None of these	13%

Q. Which of the following phrases can you say in a language other than English?
(More than one answer could be given)

Hello	85%	Two beers please	54%
Thank you	84%	How much does it cost?	50%
Goodbye	83%	The bill please	49%
Please	77%	Where is the toilet?	44%
My name is ...	68%	Do you know the way to...?	34%
Do you speak English?	64%	None of these	7%

Q. Which ONE of the following BEST describes your attitude towards foreign languages when you are on holiday abroad?

52%
I learn a few key phrases beforehand so that I can try and converse when I'm on holiday and talk to the locals. I think it's important to make an effort

13%
English is such a well known language, especially in Europe, I think everyone should speak it

12%
Learning and engaging with a foreign language is a major part of my holiday experience

7%
I rely 100% on a phrase book or online translator – I'd be lost without it but I like to at least try and speak the local language

16%
None of these

Using phrase books

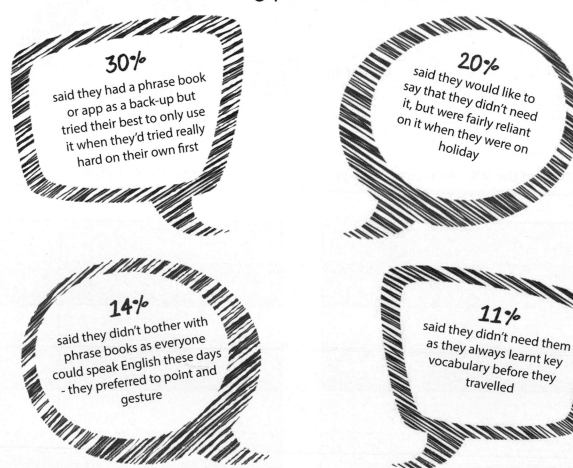

30%
said they had a phrase book or app as a back-up but tried their best to only use it when they'd tried really hard on their own first

20%
said they would like to say that they didn't need it, but were fairly reliant on it when they were on holiday

14%
said they didn't bother with phrase books as everyone could speak English these days - they preferred to point and gesture

11%
said they didn't need them as they always learnt key vocabulary before they travelled

Q. In your opinion, why is it important to have conversations in the local language when on holiday abroad?
(More than one answer could be given)

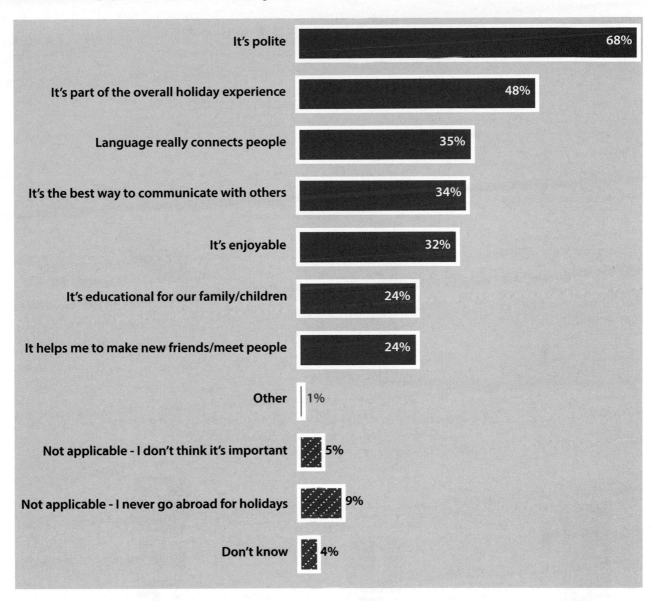

It's polite	68%
It's part of the overall holiday experience	48%
Language really connects people	35%
It's the best way to communicate with others	34%
It's enjoyable	32%
It's educational for our family/children	24%
It helps me to make new friends/meet people	24%
Other	1%
Not applicable - I don't think it's important	5%
Not applicable - I never go abroad for holidays	9%
Don't know	4%

Base: 2,042 GB adults. 96% said English was their first language - ie the language they learnt before any other

Some issues

- Only 22% of people gave a very positive answer about learning languages. Why is this?

- 48% would quite like to learn a language - what is stopping them?

- Will English eventually be the only European language?

- What are the benefits of being able to speak to people in their own language?

Source: © YouGov 2013 - Lost in Translation survey for DFDS Seaways
www.dfdsseaways.co.uk
www.yougov.co.uk

Language barriers

Many British holidaymakers struggle with languages and culture

Language skills in the UK's adult population

75%

of people in the UK say they cannot speak a foreign language well enough to hold a conversation

Q: Which, if any, of the following languages can you speak well enough to hold a conversation?

(More than one answer could be given. Base: 4,171 UK adults)

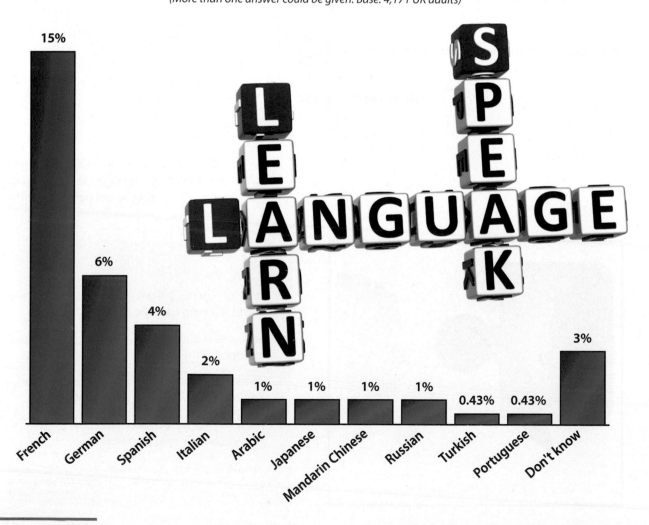

French	German	Spanish	Italian	Arabic	Japanese	Mandarin Chinese	Russian	Turkish	Portuguese	Don't know
15%	6%	4%	2%	1%	1%	1%	1%	0.43%	0.43%	3%

People who had ever done any of the following while on holiday abroad

(Base: 2,000 GB adults)

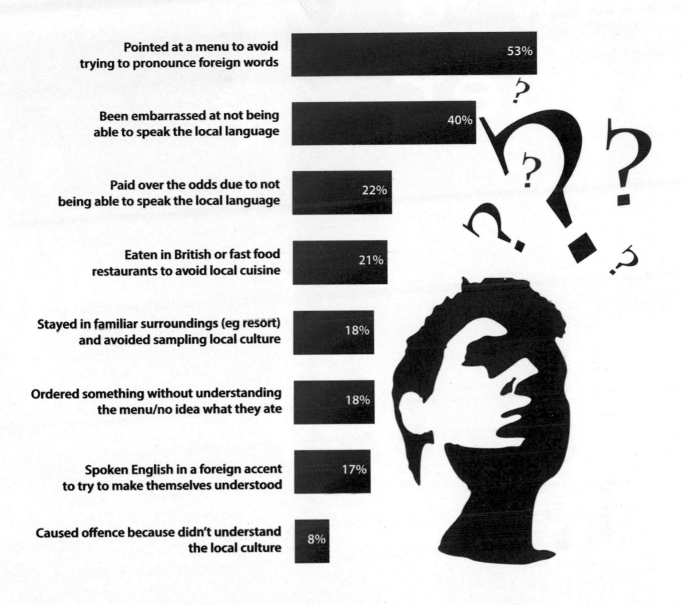

Pointed at a menu to avoid trying to pronounce foreign words	53%
Been embarrassed at not being able to speak the local language	40%
Paid over the odds due to not being able to speak the local language	22%
Eaten in British or fast food restaurants to avoid local cuisine	21%
Stayed in familiar surroundings (eg resort) and avoided sampling local culture	18%
Ordered something without understanding the menu/no idea what they ate	18%
Spoken English in a foreign accent to try to make themselves understood	17%
Caused offence because didn't understand the local culture	8%

"Too many of us have to rely on English when we're overseas. And, if not speaking the 'lingo' means we're missing out on holiday, imagine what it's costing the UK in trade and business opportunities in the longer term."

John Worne,
Director of Strategy at the British Council

Some issues

- Why don't more British people speak a foreign language?

- Which languages might be the most important in the future?

- What are the benefits of being able to speak to people in their own language?

Source: Language for the Future Report, British Council
www.britishcouncil.org

Law &
order

Violence against women

The world's biggest survey on women's experiences of violence revealed the extent of abuse suffered at home, work, in public and online

A survey of **42,000 women** aged 18-74 who live in the 28 EU Member States, found that **33%** have **experienced physical and/or sexual violence** since the age of 15. That's an estimated **62 million women.**

When the violence had taken place

(Women who had experienced physical and/or sexual violence since the age of 15)

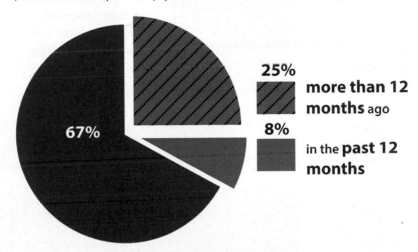

67%

25%

⬛ **more than 12 months** ago

8%

⬛ in the **past 12 months**

Physical violence

Examples of physical violence include being pushed, shoved, slapped, grabbed or kicked; had a hard object thrown at them; been beaten with a fist or a hard object; been burned, cut or stabbed; been shot at; had their head beaten against something; or had someone try to suffocate or strangle them.

An estimated **13 million women** have experienced physical violence in the **past 12 months**

Sexual violence

Examples of sexual violence include being forced or an attempt made to force them into sexual intercourse (oral, anal or vaginal); taken part in any form of sexual activity when they did not want to; or they have consented to sexual activity because they were afraid of what might happen if they refused.

An estimated **3.7 million women** have experienced sexual violence in the **past 12 months**.

Sexual harassment

55% of women have experienced some form of sexual harassment - **32%** of all victims of sexual harassment said the perpetrator was connected with work - a boss, colleague or customer.

Rape

5% of women have been raped since the age of 15. Of those women who have experienced sexual violence from someone who wasn't their partner, almost one in 10 said that more than one person was involved in the most serious incident.

Psychological violence

43% have experienced some form of psychological violence by either a current or a previous partner such as public humiliation, forbidding a woman to leave the house or locking her up, forcing her to watch pornography and threats of violence.

Stalking

Stalking: where the same person has been repeatedly offensive or threatening towards a woman eg by loitering or waiting for them or by making offensive, threatening or silent phone calls to them.

18% of women have experienced stalking since the age of 15, and **5%** of women have experienced it in the past 12 months - which amounts to an estimated **9 million women**.

21% of women who have experienced stalking said that it lasted for over 2 years.

22%
of women have experienced physical and/or sexual violence by a **partner**

Cyberharassment

11% of women have experienced inappropriate advances on social websites or have been subjected to sexually explicit emails or text messages.

The risk of becoming a target of threatening and offensive advances on the internet is twice as high for young women aged 18–29 years as for women aged 40–49 years.

Talking about violence

In different countries, it may be more or less acceptable to talk with other people about experiences of violence against women. In some societies these incidents are unlikely to be shared with family and friends and are also rarely reported to the police - therefore the figures could be higher.

Gender equality could lead to higher levels of disclosure about violence against women.

Getting help

After the most serious incident of violence, women said they wanted to have someone to talk to, to support them, protection and other practical help.

33% of victims of partner violence and **26%** of victims of non-partner violence contacted either the police or a victim support organisation, following the most serious incident of violence.

About one third of victims of partner violence have shared their experiences with someone – and had the support of their family and friends in helping them to overcome the violence.

Women may have experienced several violent incidents in a relationship before they decide to report the most serious one in an effort to stop the violence from happening again or getting worse. Non-partner violence is more likely to involve one-off incidents with less risk of it happening again.

For about **25%** of victims, feeling ashamed or embarrassed about what has happened was the reason for not reporting the most serious incident of sexual violence by a partner or a non-partner to the police or any other organisation.

Freedom

53% of women avoided certain situations or places, at least sometimes, for fear of being physically or sexually assaulted. In comparison, surveys show that far fewer men restrict their movement.

Useful organisations

Women's Aid 0808 2000 247
www.womensaid.org.uk

Respect 0808 802 4040
www.respect.uk.net

End Violence Against Women 020 7033 1559
www.endviolenceagainstwomen.org.uk

www.gov.uk/domestic-violence-and-abuse

Rape Crisis 0808 802 9999
www.rapecrisis.org.uk

Everyman Project 0207 263 8884
www.everymanproject.co.uk

Some issues

- Are these figures surprising?

- This survey covered 28 EU countries. How would cultural differences affect the figures?

- Whose problem is this? Who should act on it?

- What can be done to encourage safer, happier relationships?

Source: Violence against women: An EU-wide survey - European Union Agency for Fundamental Rights (FRA) http://fra.europa.eu

Perceptions of the police

Most young people have a positive view of the police - but age, gender and ethnicity can all make a difference

What type of opinion do 10-15 year olds have of the police?

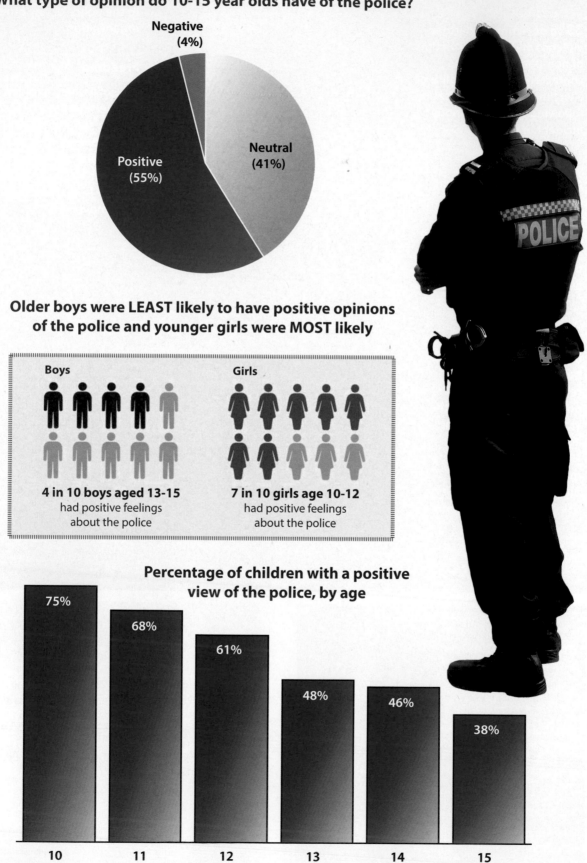

Negative
(4%)

Positive
(55%)

Neutral
(41%)

Older boys were LEAST likely to have positive opinions of the police and younger girls were MOST likely

Boys

Girls

4 in 10 boys aged 13-15
had positive feelings
about the police

7 in 10 girls age 10-12
had positive feelings
about the police

Percentage of children with a positive view of the police, by age

Age	Percentage
10	75%
11	68%
12	61%
13	48%
14	46%
15	38%

What young people think of the police

90% thought that the police would help you if you needed them.

90% thought that the police would treat you fairly if they stopped and searched you.

87% thought that the police treated each race and religion fairly.

75% thought that the police are helpful and friendly to young people.

71% thought that the police understood young people's problems in the area.

67% thought that the police dealt with things that mattered to local young people.

45% thought that the police treated young people the same as adults.

Reasons young people had contact with the police

22% of all the young people asked had been approached by the police - they said the most common reasons were:

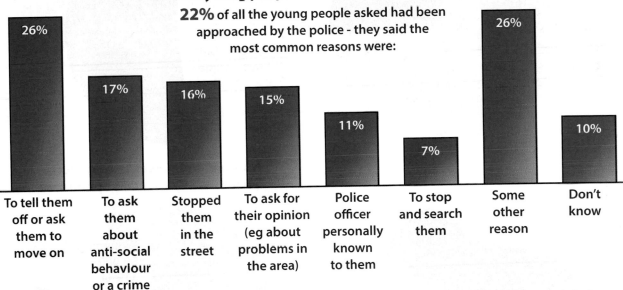

To tell them off or ask them to move on	To ask them about anti-social behaviour or a crime	Stopped them in the street	To ask for their opinion (eg about problems in the area)	Police officer personally known to them	To stop and search them	Some other reason	Don't know
26%	17%	16%	15%	11%	7%	26%	10%

Race characteristics

The largest difference in agreement between **White** respondents and **non-White** respondents was with the statement *"police treat everyone fairly whatever their skin colour or religion"*. **White** respondents were more likely to agree - **90%**, than **non-White** respondents - **77%**.

Satisfaction with the police

78% of those who had been approached by the police were **satisfied** with the way it had been handled. **8%** were **neither satisfied nor dissatisfied** and **14%** were **dissatisfied**.

Some issues

- How close are these figures to your own opinions?

- Do you think the figures would change if the same questions were put to an older age group?

- What sort of things would make a difference to your opinion about the police?

- Why do you think race and gender affects people's opinion of the police?

Base: 2,879 young people aged 10 to 15 in England & Wales

Source: 10 to 15 Year Olds' Perceptions of the Police - Crime Survey for England & Wales 2012/13. Office for National Statistics © Crown copyright 2014 www.ons.gov.uk

Inequality in sport

Is sport sexist? There are still huge differences in male and female earnings

Some examples of differences between men's and women's versions of a sport:

Gymnastics: Women compete in **four** events: vault, uneven bars, balance beam and floor - to music. The emphasis is on grace and flexibility.

Men have **six** events: floor, pommel horse, rings, vault, bars and high bar. The emphasis is on strength and power.

Boxing, Wrestling, Weightlifting: There are more weight divisions in Olympic men's boxing, wrestling and weightlifting than in the women's side of the sport.

Cycling: Female riders want equality in pay, equality in prize money and equality in racing – women can race up to 140km a day on the road while men are allowed to ride 280km.

Swimming: Currently the men's and women's Olympic schedules both contain 17 events with the only difference being men swim 1500m while women compete over 800m.

Tennis: While men play five sets at Grand Slams, women can only compete over three.

"Not having some of these sporting events for women is just inertia from a time when it was believed women weren't sturdy enough for serious training and competition."

David Epstein, sports writer

Athletics: The men's decathlon has been contested at every Olympics since 1912. But there is still no place at major championships for the women's event.

Lacrosse: Women's lacrosse started in 1890 - only stick contact was allowed and this has not changed over the years, but men are allowed full body and stick contact. In 2014 the sport's lawmakers agreed to make the field size for men and women equal.

Diving: Women take five dives, men six.

Shooting: There are no women's events in the rapid fire or 50m pistol, nor at Olympic level in the double trap or 50m rifle prone.

Bobsleigh: Women's bobsleigh became an Olympic sport in 2002 as a two-person event, while the men continued to race two-man and four-man sleighs. In September 2014 the governing body for bobsleigh agreed to allow four-woman bobsleigh races.

Men get more prize money than women in **30%** of sports.

Football World Cup: men are paid **nearly 40 times** more than women.

Cricket World Cup: men are paid **over 50 times more** than women.

Out of **35** sports that pay prize money, only **25** pay equally.

Tennis was the first sport to pay equal prize money in 1973 after campaigning from Billie Jean King and other female tennis players.

By 2004, athletics, bowls, skating, marathons, shooting and volleyball had also started to pay equal prize money.

Diving, sailing, taekwondo, windsurfing and some cycling events have started to pay equal prize money in the past couple of years.

Sports with the biggest difference in prize money between men and women

Sport	Men's prize money	Women's prize money
Football Premier League/Women's Super League	£24m	0
Football World Cup	£22m	£630,000
Football Champions League	£8.3m	£199,000
Cricket World Cup	£2.5m	£47,000
Football FA Cup	£1.8m	£5,000
Golf PGA	£1.1m	£212,000
Golf - The Open	£975,000	£298,000
Cricket T20 World Cup	£690,000	£44,000
Golf - US Open	£1m	£452,000
Snooker World Championship*	£300,000	£1,500
Darts BDO World Championship*	£100,000	£12,000
Surfing World Championship tour	£62,700	£37,600
Squash World Championship	£28,600	£12,300
Cliff diving world series	£12,700	£3,100
Ski jumping World Cup	£6,600	£2,000

*Main competitions open to men and women

Kelly Simmons, the Football Association's director of the national game and women's football said:

"The men's game is a huge multi-million pound industry so when you compare it to the women's game, which until three or four years ago was played by amateurs, the gulf is enormous."

73% of fun runners raised money for a cause in the last twelve months

AVERAGE AMOUNT RAISED BY RUNNERS: £280 EACH... BUT MEN RAISE MORE THAN WOMEN

Female fundraising £212

Male fundraising £369

19% of men that ran raised more than £500 in the last year compared to just 5% of women runners.

FINISH

"Running can get you fit and give you a sense of wellbeing, but few things are as rewarding as supporting a cause you really care about."

John Low
Chief Executive of the Charities Aid Foundation

Base: 2,022 members of the public across the UK

Some issues

- Why do you think numbers have increased?

- Does raising money encourage you to train more?

- Have you or would you take part in a charity run?

Source: ComRes survey for Charities Aid Foundation (CAF)
www.cafonline.org and CAF infographic
www.cafonline.org/PDF/CAF_Marathon_Infographic.pdf

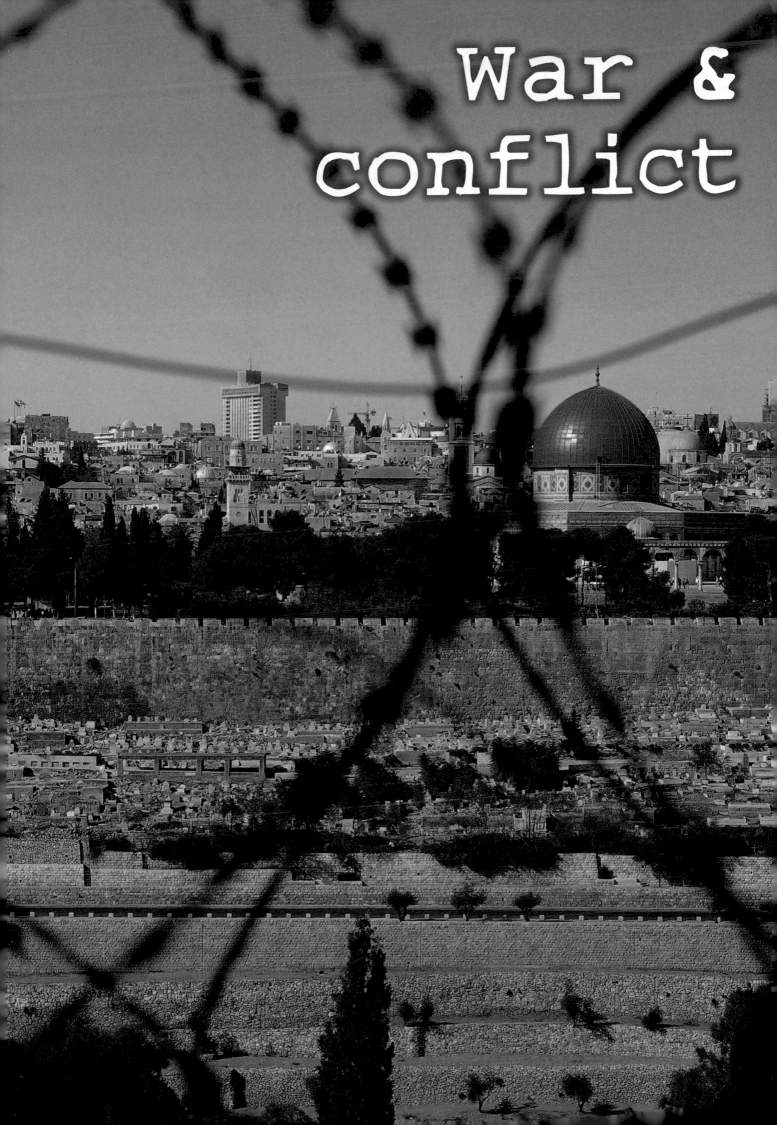

War & conflict

Afghanistan: Final toll

The cost of the Afghan war

British troops ended their combat operation on 26th October 2014

Coalition military fatalities, by year

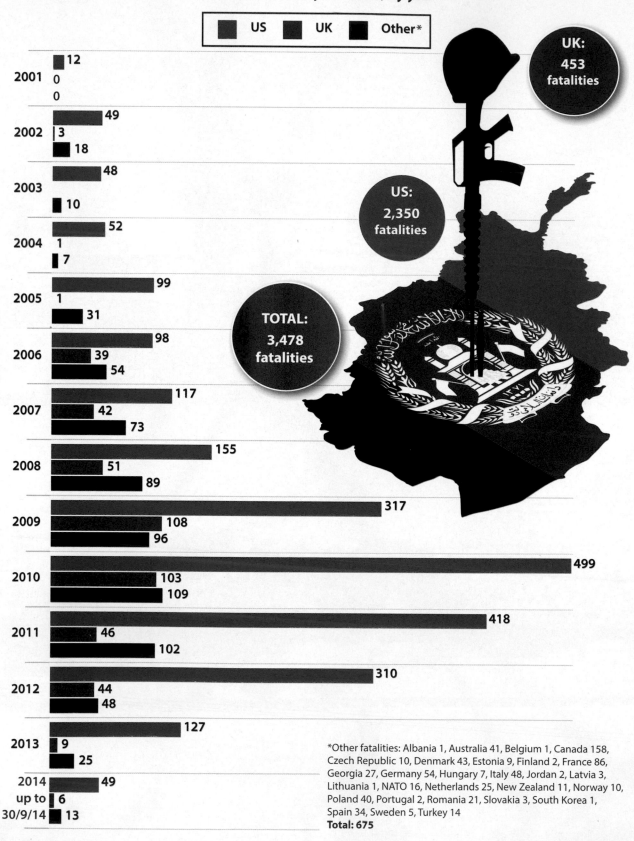

Legend: US | UK | Other*

UK: 453 fatalities

US: 2,350 fatalities

TOTAL: 3,478 fatalities

Year	US	UK	Other
2001	12	0	0
2002	49	3	18
2003	48		10
2004	52	1	7
2005	99	1	31
2006	98	39	54
2007	117	42	73
2008	155	51	89
2009	317	108	96
2010	499	103	109
2011	418	46	102
2012	310	44	48
2013	127	9	25
2014 up to 30/9/14	49	6	13

*Other fatalities: Albania 1, Australia 41, Belgium 1, Canada 158, Czech Republic 10, Denmark 43, Estonia 9, Finland 2, France 86, Georgia 27, Germany 54, Hungary 7, Italy 48, Jordan 2, Latvia 3, Lithuania 1, NATO 16, Netherlands 25, New Zealand 11, Norway 10, Poland 40, Portugal 2, Romania 21, Slovakia 3, South Korea 1, Spain 34, Sweden 5, Turkey 14
Total: 675

UK military deaths, by age
up to 30/9/14

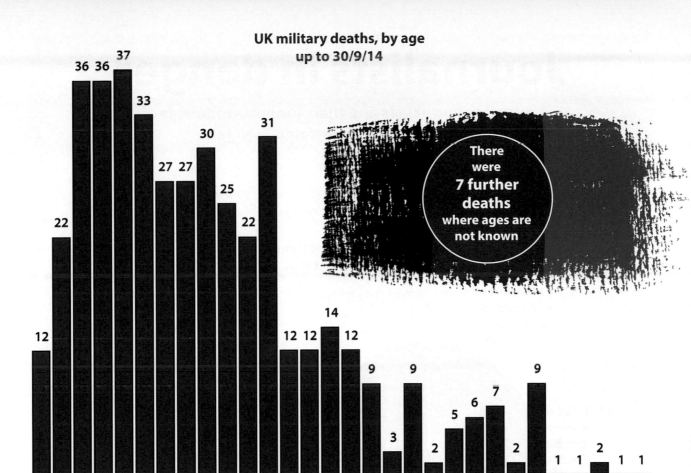

There were **7 further deaths** where ages are not known

18 19 20 21 22 23 24 25 26 27 28 29 30 31 32 33 34 35 36 37 38 39 40 41 42 43 44 48 49 51

According to a poll of 2,004 British adults:

46% felt British troops should never have been sent to Afghanistan

17% said it was right to send them but they should have returned sooner

19% believed it was right but now is the right time for troops to return

6% felt British troops should stay there for the foreseeable future

12% say they don't know

The cost of war

It is estimated that there have been more than **21,000** Afghnani **civilian casualties** since counting began in 2007 (estimates of the number of civilians killed vary widely and must be treated with caution).

In the first 6 months of 2014 there were:

4,853 civilian casualties (**1,564** killed and **3,289** injured); **1,071 child** civilian casualties (**295** killed and **776** injured); and **440 women** civilian casualties (**148** killed and **292** injured).

The operational cost to the UK government is thought to be around **£19bn** - about **£300** for every person in the UK.

Some issues

- Do you think the combat has been a success?
- How do you measure the success of a military operation?
- Do you know why the British and US troops were in Afghanistan?
- At what point does the cost of a war become unacceptable - in terms of both finance and loss of life?
- What is worth fighting for?

Source: Enduring Freedom, icasualties.org www.icasualties.org
Ministry of Defence www.army.mod.uk
ComRes/ITV News Index poll
www.comres.co.uk/poll/1304/itv-news-index-eu-and-afghanistan.htm
United Nations Assistance Mission in Afghanistan UNAMA Protection of
Civilians, July 2014 http://unama.unmissions.org

Journalists in danger

Every year journalists and their support workers face serious dangers while doing their jobs

Journalists are defined as people who cover the news or comment on public affairs through any media, such as in print, in photographs, on radio, on television, and online.

Journalist killed as a result of their work between 1992 and 31st October 2014

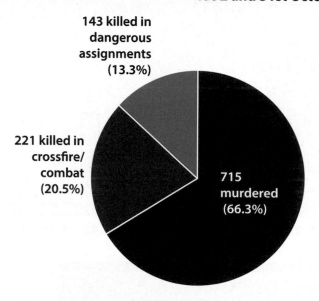

143 killed in dangerous assignments (13.3%)

221 killed in crossfire/ combat (20.5%)

715 murdered (66.3%)

These **1,079** deaths are classed as **work-related** because it is reasonably certain that the journalist was killed because of his or her work; in crossfire; or while carrying out a dangerous assignment.

There were a further **422** deaths with unclear motives, but which have a potential link to journalism - these are classed as 'unconfirmed'.

20 countries with the highest number of journalist deaths 1992-2014

Iraq: 103	Turkey: 18
Philippines: 75	Rwanda: 17
Algeria: 58	Tajikistan: 14
Colombia: 41	Bangladesh: 14
Somalia: 36	Afghanistan: 12
Russia: 36	Syria: 10
Pakistan: 32	Sri Lanka: 10
Brazil: 27	Sierra Leone: 9
Mexico: 27	Nigeria: 8
India: 19	Peru: 8

Award-winning American journalist, Marie Colvin, worked for the Sunday Times from 1985 until her death on 22 February 2012, while covering the siege of Homs in Syria.

Media workers are people who work with journalists in
supporting roles such as drivers, interpreters, fixers and guards.

Media support workers killed between 2003 and September 2014

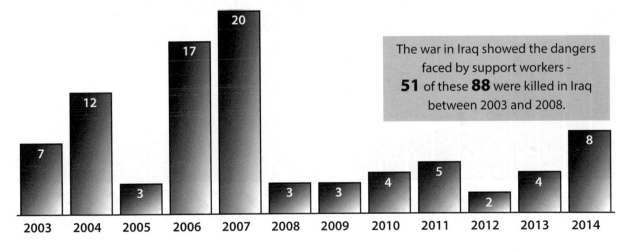

The war in Iraq showed the dangers
faced by support workers -
51 of these **88** were killed in Iraq
between 2003 and 2008.

2003	2004	2005	2006	2007	2008	2009	2010	2011	2012	2013	2014
7	12	3	17	20	3	3	4	5	2	4	8

Militants and the media

American freelance journalists James Foley and Steven Sotloff were abducted and murdered in Syria in 2014 by Islamist militants known as ISIS (Islamic State of Iraq and Syria).

ISIS issued videos of the beheadings, claiming that they were in retaliation for US air strikes. This can be seen as part of a sophisticated social media campaign to recruit fighters (especially among Westerners), to spread propaganda and to gain financial support.

Social media is being used to show us war from the viewpoint of both the victims and the aggressors.

Some issues

* Why are journalists in so much danger?

* How do the internet and technology help or hinder accurate reporting?

* Why does journalism matter?

Source: Committee to Protect Journalists www.cpj.org

Journalists in prison

Turkey, Iran and China accounted for more than half of all journalists imprisoned around the world in 2013

Charges

Worldwide, **124** journalists were jailed on 'anti-state' charges such as undermining the authority or structure of power in that country or terrorism. In **45** cases, no charges were disclosed at all.

Prison census:
Snapshot of those journalists recorded to be in prison on 1st December each year
(It does not include the many journalists imprisoned and released throughout the year)

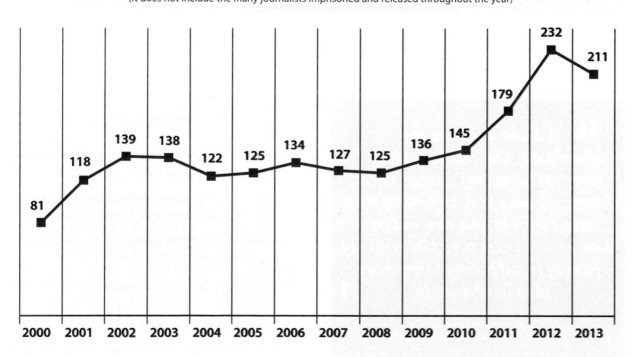

2000	2001	2002	2003	2004	2005	2006	2007	2008	2009	2010	2011	2012	2013
81	118	139	138	122	125	134	127	125	136	145	179	232	211

Despite each having released some prisoners during 2013, Turkey and Iran remained the worst and second worst jailers for two years in a row.

Number of journalists imprisoned on 1st December 2013 and country held
The top 10 worst jailers of journalists

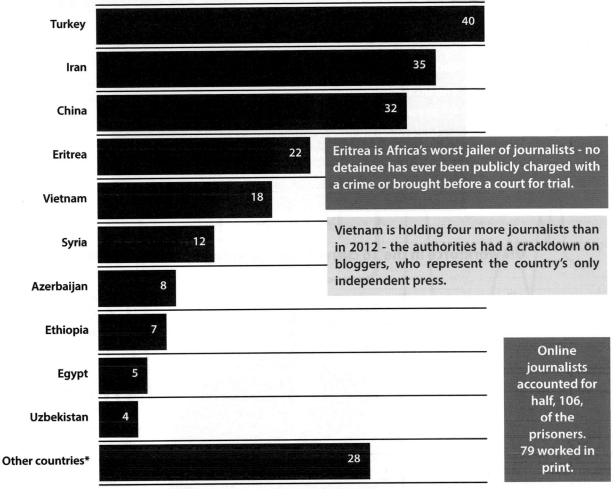

Country	Number
Turkey	40
Iran	35
China	32
Eritrea	22
Vietnam	18
Syria	12
Azerbaijan	8
Ethiopia	7
Egypt	5
Uzbekistan	4
Other countries*	28

Eritrea is Africa's worst jailer of journalists - no detainee has ever been publicly charged with a crime or brought before a court for trial.

Vietnam is holding four more journalists than in 2012 - the authorities had a crackdown on bloggers, who represent the country's only independent press.

Online journalists accounted for half, 106, of the prisoners. 79 worked in print.

*Other countries include:
Israel & the Occupied Palestinian Territories 3, Bahrain 3, Jordan 2, Russia 2, Saudi Arabia 2, Somalia 2, Bangladesh 1, Democratic Republic of Congo 1, Gambia 1, India 1, Italy 1, Kuwait 1, Kyrgyzstan 1, Macedonia 1, Morocco 1, Pakistan 1, Republic of Congo 1, Rwanda 1, Thailand 1, United States 1

Missing

Journalists who either disappear or are abducted by criminal gangs or militant groups are not included in the prison figures - their cases are classified as 'missing' or 'abducted'.

Around 38 journalists are listed as missing since 1982, ie disappeared while doing their work. Although some of them are feared dead, no bodies have been found, and they are therefore not classified as "killed."

Cases of journalists missing in Syria are extremely difficult to track. Information is scarce, the situation is constantly changing, and some cases go unreported.

Some issues

- Why do some states lock up journalists?

- How would journalists undermine authority?

- Why do journalists continue to do their job in difficult circumstances?

- How important is it to have a free press?

Source: Committee to Protect Journalists www.cpj.org

War & peace

A snapshot of the state of peace around the world

The Global Peace Index (GPI) measures conflict **inside countries** and **between countries**, **safety and security in society** and **military build-up** in a country. It ranks **162** countries according to their 'absence of violence'.

Overall the world has become less peaceful.

Since 2008, **111** countries have become less peaceful while only **51** have become more peaceful.

MOST peaceful
1st

ICELAND

1	Iceland
2	Denmark
3	Austria
4	New Zealand
5	Switzerland
6	Finland
7	Canada
8	Japan
9	Belgium
10	Norway

LEAST peaceful
162nd

SYRIA

153	North Korea
154	Pakistan
155	Dem. Rep. of Congo
156	Central African Republic
157	Sudan
158	Somalia
159	Iraq
160	South Sudan
161	Afghanistan
162	Syria

The **UK** ranks **47th.** This is because of involvement in overseas conflicts, such as Afghanistan and because the UK has substantial armed forces and weapons.

Europe remained the most peaceful region in the world due to its lack of conflicts.

Afghanistan has been replaced at the bottom of the Index by Syria because Afghanistan has seen a slight improvement in its peace while Syria's civil war has intensified over the last year. An estimated 100,000 people have been killed in Syria since the fighting erupted in 2011.

Syria was worst because of: the number of refugees and displaced persons (estimated at over one-third of the population); access to small arms and light weapons; and overall level of violent crime.

Some issues

- Do you think the Peace Index tells us anything about the state of the world?

- Is it measuring the right things?

- How can the world be made more peaceful?

- Can you understand why the UK is ranked 47th, even though there is little conflict in the country?

Source: Global Peace Index 2014 - The Institute for Economics and Peace (IEP) www.economicsandpeace.org

Wider
world

Force of nature

Natural disasters hit 108 countries in 2013

	Disaster types	Examples
Natural Disaster: an unforeseen and often sudden event that causes great damage, destruction and human suffering eg flooding or earthquake	**Climatological** events caused by long term climate processes	Extreme temperature, drought, wildfire
	Geophysical events originating from solid earth	Earthquake, volcano, rockfall
	Hydrological events caused by abnormal water behaviour	Flood, avalanches, landslides
	Meteorological events caused by short term weather processes	Storms

Top 10 countries by number of reported events, 2013

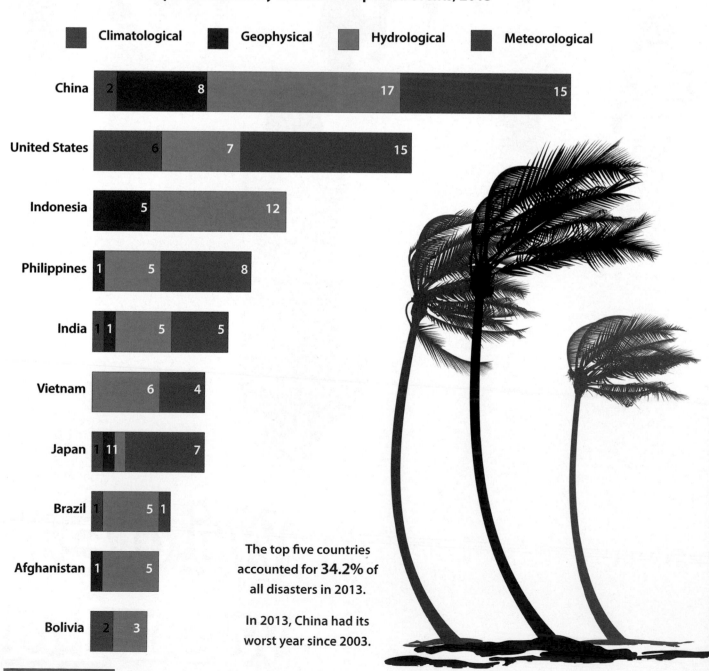

■ Climatological ■ Geophysical ■ Hydrological ■ Meteorological

China 2 | 8 | 17 | 15

United States 6 | 7 | 15

Indonesia 5 | 12

Philippines 1 | 5 | 8

India 1 | 1 | 5 | 5

Vietnam 6 | 4

Japan 1 | 11 | 7

Brazil 1 | 5 | 1

Afghanistan 1 | 5

Bolivia 2 | 3

The top five countries accounted for **34.2%** of all disasters in 2013.

In 2013, China had its worst year since 2003.

Impact of disasters

In 2013, the impact of disasters on humans was at its **lowest level in 16 years**. However, a huge number of people were still affected.

Worldwide, the **330 natural disasters** caused the **DEATHS** of more than **21,610 people**, created **96.5 million VICTIMS** and caused a record amount of **DAMAGES - US$ 118.6 billion**.

Disasters which caused the most DEATHS in 2013

Disaster	Country	Number of deaths
Tropical cyclone (Haiyan)	Philippines	7,354
Flood	India	6,054
Heatwave	UK	760
Heatwave	India	557
Earthquake	Pakistan	399

Top 5 countries affected by natural disasters in 2013, by different categories

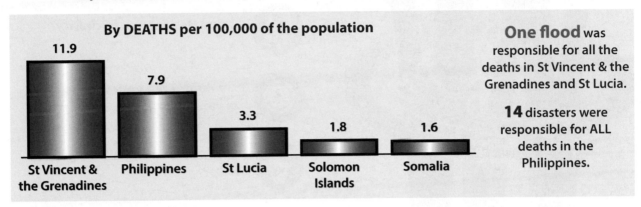

By DEATHS per 100,000 of the population

- St Vincent & the Grenadines: 11.9
- Philippines: 7.9
- St Lucia: 3.3
- Solomon Islands: 1.8
- Somalia: 1.6

One flood was responsible for all the deaths in St Vincent & the Grenadines and St Lucia.

14 disasters were responsible for ALL deaths in the Philippines.

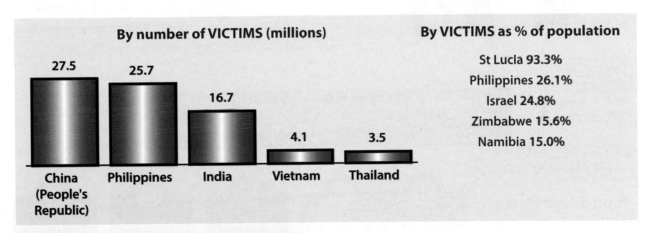

By number of VICTIMS (millions)

- China (People's Republic): 27.5
- Philippines: 25.7
- India: 16.7
- Vietnam: 4.1
- Thailand: 3.5

By VICTIMS as % of population

- St Lucia 93.3%
- Philippines 26.1%
- Israel 24.8%
- Zimbabwe 15.6%
- Namibia 15.0%

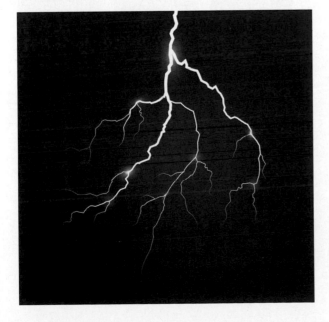

Some issues

- Can anything be done to prevent natural disasters?

- How should the rest of the world react when a country has suffered a devastating disaster?

- What can the global population do to prepare for natural disasters?

Source: Annual Disaster Statistical Review 2013– The numbers and trends, Centre for Research on the Epidemiology of Disasters (CRED) September 2014 www.cred.be

World Giving Index

A global view of giving trends

The World Giving Index surveys **over 155,000 people** in **135 countries**, which represents around **94%** of the world's population.

They were asked about three aspects of giving: **In the past month have you ...**

 ...donated money to charity?

 ...volunteered your time to an organisation?

 ...helped a stranger who needed help?

The survey averages the responses from the three key questions, each country is given a percentage and then ranked in order based on their score.

The **United States** is top overall in the World Giving Index, 2013 - its score of **61%** is the highest on record.

Top 10 most giving nations

	World Giving Index ranking	World Giving Index score (%)	Donating money score (%)	Volunteering time score (%)	Helping a stranger score (%)
United States of America	1	61	62	45	77
Canada	2	58	68	42	64
Myanmar	2	58	85	43	46
New Zealand	2	58	67	40	67
Ireland	5	57	70	37	64
United Kingdom	6	57	76	29	65
Australia	7	55	67	34	64
Netherlands	8	54	69	37	57
Qatar	9	51	60	19	73
Sri Lanka	10	48	45	46	54

Globally, the United States ranks: **1st** for **helping a stranger**, **3rd** for **volunteering time**, and **13th** for **donating money**.

Donating Money

Highest-ranked countries by PERCENTAGE of people who donate money to charity in a typical month

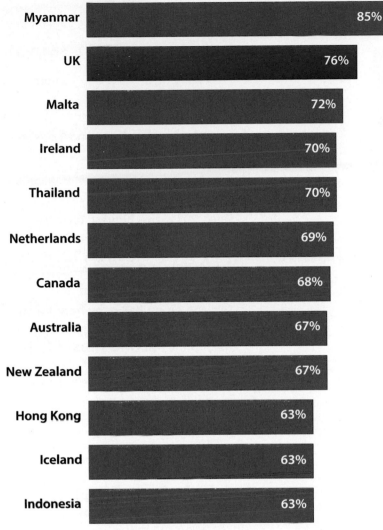

Country	Percentage
Myanmar	85%
UK	76%
Malta	72%
Ireland	70%
Thailand	70%
Netherlands	69%
Canada	68%
Australia	67%
New Zealand	67%
Hong Kong	63%
Iceland	63%
Indonesia	63%

Although the United States is at the top of the **overall** World Giving Index rankings, it does not feature in the top ten countries for the percentage of people donating money. It comes second in the number of people donating.

More people donated money to charity in **India** than anywhere else in the world.

NUMBER of people donating money

Highest ranked country	People (millions)
India	244
USA	158
China	113
Indonesia	110
Pakistan	45
UK	39
Thailand	38
Brazil	34
Germany	34
Myanmar	34

Volunteering

Highest-ranked countries by PERCENTAGE of people volunteering time in a typical month

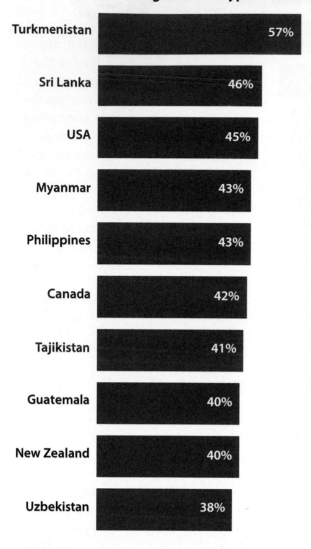

Country	Percentage
Turkmenistan	57%
Sri Lanka	46%
USA	45%
Myanmar	43%
Philippines	43%
Canada	42%
Tajikistan	41%
Guatemala	40%
New Zealand	40%
Uzbekistan	38%

UK

The UK ranked **26th** with **29%** of people volunteering time.

Gender

Globally **21.1%** of men and **18.4%** of women volunteered.

Age

Since 2011, the biggest increase in volunteering has occurred among **15-24 year olds** (from **18.4%** in 2011 to **20.6%** in 2012).

This age group has gone from being the **least likely** to volunteer in 2008 to the **second most likely** to volunteer in 2012.

NUMBER of people volunteering time

Highest ranked country	People (millions)
India	157
USA	115
Indonesia	52
China	45
Nigeria	34
Philippines	27
Mexico	21
Russia	21
Brazil	19
Germany	19

Helping a stranger

Highest-ranked countries by PERCENTAGE of people who helped a stranger in a typical month

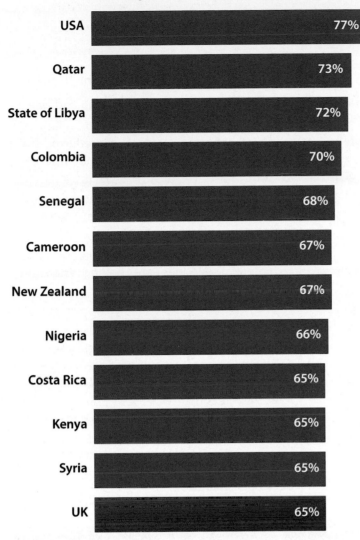

Country	Percentage
USA	77%
Qatar	73%
State of Libya	72%
Colombia	70%
Senegal	68%
Cameroon	67%
New Zealand	67%
Nigeria	66%
Costa Rica	65%
Kenya	65%
Syria	65%
UK	65%

The number of people who **helped others grew by** **over 200 million**; more than double the growth in the number of people donating money and volunteering.

NUMBER of people who helped a stranger

Highest ranked country	People (millions)
China	373
India	253
USA	197
Indonesia	70
Brazil	63
Nigeria	62
Pakistan	60
Bangladesh	53
Germany	40
Russia	40

Some issues

- Why is it important to have both a number and a percentage in order to rank nations?

- Does an index like this tell us anything about national characteristics?

- Is the survey a good indicator of how generous people are with their money and time?

Source: World Giving Index 2013, Charities Aid Foundation, 2013
www.cafonline.org

Ebola: The facts

The 2014 epidemic has killed more people than all other known Ebola outbreaks combined

What is it?

Ebola virus disease (EVD) is a severe, often fatal illness in humans. It was first identified in 1976.

The 2014 outbreak in West Africa has mainly affected Guinea, Liberia and Sierra Leone - these three countries have had long periods of war and instability leaving them with very weak health systems.

How does it spread?

- People can become infected if they come into contact with the blood, body fluids or organs of an infected person. This means that most people are infected when they are caring for others, for example parents, relatives, health workers.

- People remain infectious as long as their blood and body fluids contain the virus.

- Around 50% of people who catch Ebola die from it.

- Burial ceremonies in which mourners have direct contact with the body can also spread infection.

Prevention and control

- Simply washing hands with soap and water can destroy the virus.

- Strict infection control procedures and wearing protective clothing minimise the risk.

- In developed countries, patients diagnosed with Ebola virus disease are placed in isolation in intensive care.

- There is no proven treatment but two potential vaccines are being tested on humans.

British Survivor

William Pooley was the first British person to catch Ebola when he was working as a volunteer nurse in Sierra Leone. He was treated in the UK with the experimental drug ZMapp which had not been tested on humans. He donated his blood for medical research.

He returned to Sierra Leone to continue his work and has recently called for increased aid from developed countries.

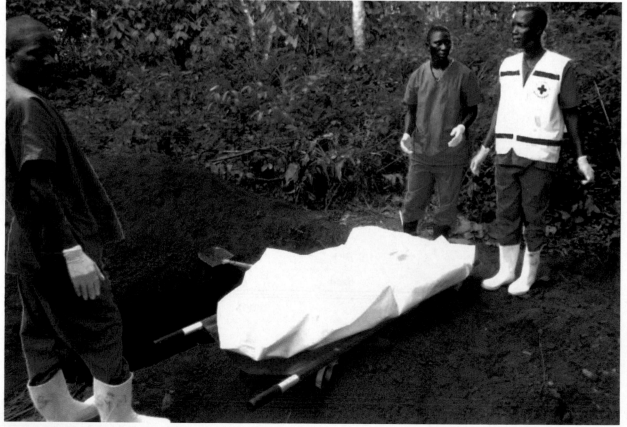

Photo: ©EC/ECHO/Jean-Louis Mosser

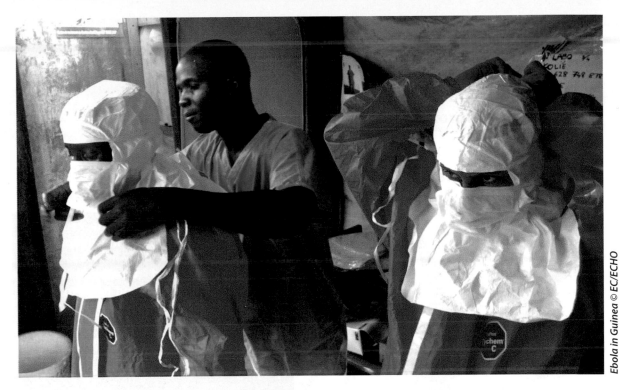

Ebola in Guinea © EC/ECHO

Confirmed, probable, and suspected cases of Ebola and reported deaths, 12th November 2014

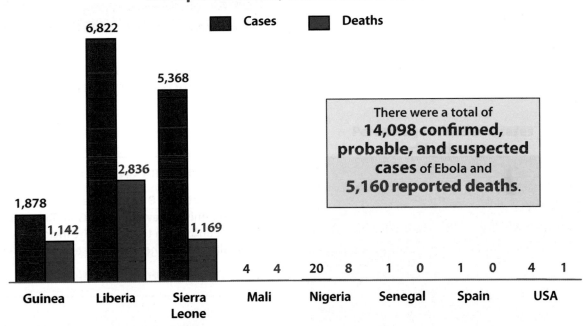

■ Cases   ■ Deaths

	Cases	Deaths
Guinea	1,878	1,142
Liberia	6,822	2,836
Sierra Leone	5,368	1,169
Mali	4	4
Nigeria	20	8
Senegal	1	0
Spain	1	0
USA	4	1

There were a total of **14,098 confirmed, probable, and suspected cases** of Ebola and **5,160 reported deaths**.

Health-care workers at risk

A total of **549** health-care workers were known to have been **infected** with Ebola up to the end of 4th November 2014:

88 in **Guinea**;
318 in **Liberia**;
11 in **Nigeria**;
128 in **Sierra Leone**;
1 in **Spain**; and
3 in the **USA** (two were infected in the USA and one in Guinea).

A total of **311** health-care workers have died.

Some issues

- There are very few risks to people in the developed world yet there is a lot of fear of Ebola. Why is that?

- Comment on this statement: 'The reason people in the West are concerned about Ebola and not about poverty is because you can't catch poverty'.

- What could prevent such outbreaks in the future?

Source: WHO www.who.int BBC News www.bbc.co.uk

Malaria deaths

Estimated number of malaria deaths worldwide

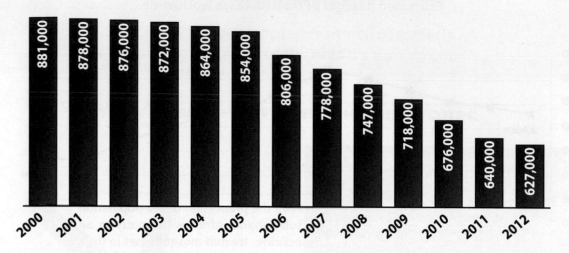

Year	Deaths
2000	881,000
2001	878,000
2002	876,000
2003	872,000
2004	864,000
2005	854,000
2006	806,000
2007	778,000
2008	747,000
2009	718,000
2010	676,000
2011	640,000
2012	627,000

If this rate of decrease continues, by 2015 malaria deaths will decrease globally in all age groups by 56%. In under fives the decrease will be 63%

Estimated number of deaths per WHO region 2000 & 2012

WHO regions	2000	2012
African	802,000	562,000
Americas	2,100	800
Eastern Mediterranean	22,000	18,000
European	3	0
South-East Asia	49,000	42,000
Western Pacific	6,900	3,500
World	881,000	627,000

About 40% of malaria deaths occur in just two countries: **Nigeria** and the **Democratic Republic of the Congo**

Percentage of malaria deaths worldwide 2012

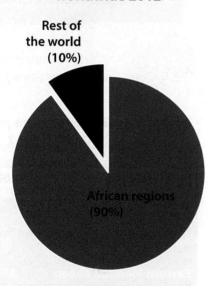

Rest of the world (10%)

African regions (90%)

Cost of control

International funding towards controlling malaria rose from **$100m** in **2000** to **$1.97** billion in **2013**.

An estimated **$5.1 billion** is needed every year but in 2012 funding only amounted to **$2.5 billion**, less than half of what is needed.

Some issues

- Why do you think funding for controlling malaria has not reached the full amount needed?

- Africa has 80% of cases but an even higher proportion of deaths. Why do you think this is?

- Can malaria be completely defeated?

Source: World Malaria Report 2013 © WHO
www.who.int/malaria/en
www.who.int/features/factfiles/malaria/en

Young people

Who do you admire?

The most inspirational figures for young people in the UK

1,013 young people aged 16-24 were surveyed for the Starbucks Youth Inspiration Index about who they admired in the public eye and why.

The Index was made up of a number of stages of research to create a list of inspirational people from fields such as polltics, sports and entertainment.

The figures on the list were then rated in 19 categories, for example, whether they cared about social issues; their involvement in charitable or volunteer work; their positive impact on society; whether they worked hard to get where they are.

Inspirational over-40s

89% of under-25s admired the achievements of the over-40s over those of their own age group.

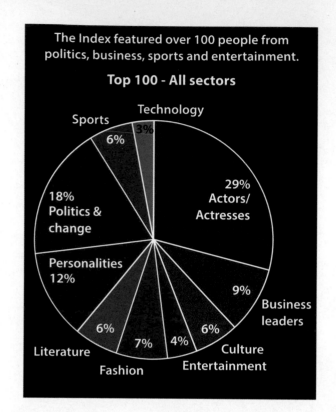

The Index featured over 100 people from politics, business, sports and entertainment.

Top 100 - All sectors

- Technology 3%
- Sports 6%
- 29% Actors/Actresses
- 18% Politics & change
- 9% Business leaders
- Personalities 12%
- 6% Culture
- Literature 6%
- Fashion 7%
- 4% Entertainment

Most inspiring Britons, by gender

TOP 5 LIVING MEN

1. STEPHEN HAWKING
2. STEPHEN FRY
3. MO FARAH
4. SIR RICHARD BRANSON
5. DAVID ATTENBOROUGH

TOP 5 LIVING WOMEN

1. JESSICA ENNIS-HILL
2. J.K. ROWLING
3. CLARE BALDING
4. REBECCA ADLINGTON
5. DAME JUDI DENCH

Q. Who has worked hard to get where they are?
Top 5 answers

95%	91%	89%	89%	88%
mentioned Jessica Ennis-Hill	mentioned Mo Farah	mentioned Ryan Gosling	mentioned JK Rowling	mentioned Rebecca Adlington

Q. Who seems genuine?
Top 5 answers

95%	91%	89%	88%	85%
mentloned Mo Farah	mentioned Dame Judi Dench	mentioned Jessica Ennis-Hill	mentioned Rebecca Adlington	mentioned Bob Marley

Q. Who has made good decisions?
Top 5 answers

92%	91%	87%	86%	85%
mentioned Mo Farah	mentioned Jessica Ennis-Hill	mentioned Sir Richard Branson	mentioned Dame Judi Dench	mentioned Steven Spielberg

Inspirational women

37% of the top 25 role models are women: Ellen DeGeneres, Dame Judi Dench, JK Rowling and Rebecca Adlington all rank highly for their hard work, dedication and genuine approach.

"It's exciting to see so many successful women viewed as inspirational to the youth of today."

Rebecca Adlington
(the only under 25 nominated)

Some issues

- Are you surprised by some of the choices?

- Why do sports people figure so prominently in the Top Five lists?

- What characteristics of the Top 5 living men and the Top 5 living women make them good choices?

- Only 37% of the top 25 role models are women. Why do you think there Isn't a more equal split along gender lines?

Source: Starbucks Inspiration Index 2104, Starbucks Youth Action 2014, UK Youth
www.starbucks.co.uk/responsibility/community/youth-action
www.ukyouth.org

How do you feel?

Unemployment, underachievement at school or growing up in poverty can have a big impact on the overall wellbeing of young people

Unemployment

Mental health problems which have been experienced by long-term unemployed respondents compared to all young people

Symptom	Long-term unemployed (out of work for 6 months or more)	All young people
I have been prescribed anti-depressants	25%	11%
I have experienced panic attacks	29%	22%
I have had trouble sleeping	39%	37%
I have felt suicidal	32%	26%
I have self-harmed	24%	19%
I have had difficulty controlling my anger	25%	20%
I take drugs	12%	8%

9% of all young people believe they have "nothing to live for".
This rises to 21% among the long-term unemployed.

" Seeing friends talk about their jobs and social lives on Facebook made me feel like there was something wrong with me. "

Emma Reilly who has now set up a design business with the support of the Prince's Trust

Photo posed by model

Underachievement at school

Young people who struggled at school are more likely to face depression

■ Young people with fewer than five GCSEs graded A*-C or Scottish Standard grades levels 1 or 2   ■ All young people

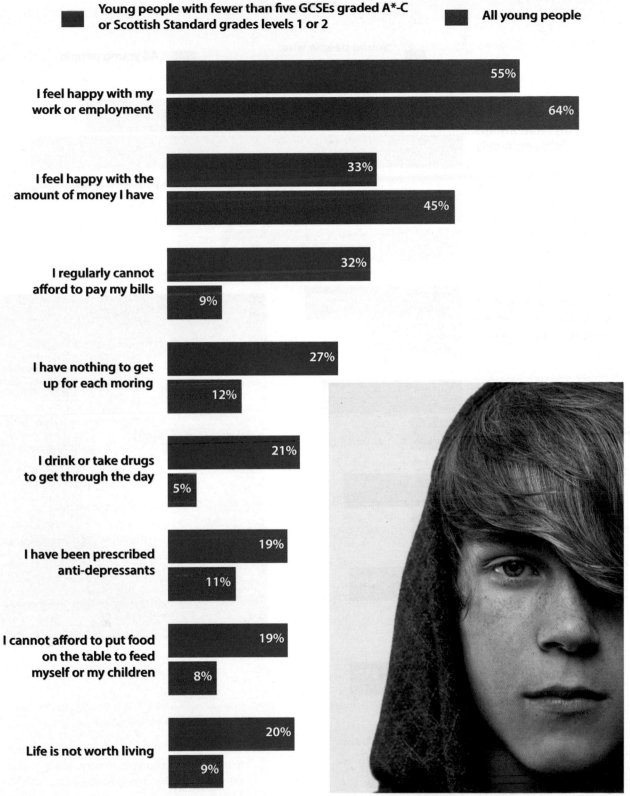

I feel happy with my work or employment
- 55%
- 64%

I feel happy with the amount of money I have
- 33%
- 45%

I regularly cannot afford to pay my bills
- 32%
- 9%

I have nothing to get up for each moring
- 27%
- 12%

I drink or take drugs to get through the day
- 21%
- 5%

I have been prescribed anti-depressants
- 19%
- 11%

I cannot afford to put food on the table to feed myself or my children
- 19%
- 8%

Life is not worth living
- 20%
- 9%

Photo posed by model

Steve Hardie was unemployed for eight years and suffered from depression and anxiety on a daily basis:

"Being out of work knocked my confidence and made me feel like a failure."

Steve got in touch with the Prince's Trust and joined their Team programme:

"I am really proud of the fact that I'm helping others, and having a job has given me back my sense of self worth."

Growing up in poverty

Thousands of young people growing up in the UK's poorest families are facing an increased risk of mental health problems and "losing" their childhoods

■ **Young people who grew up in poverty** ■ **All young people**

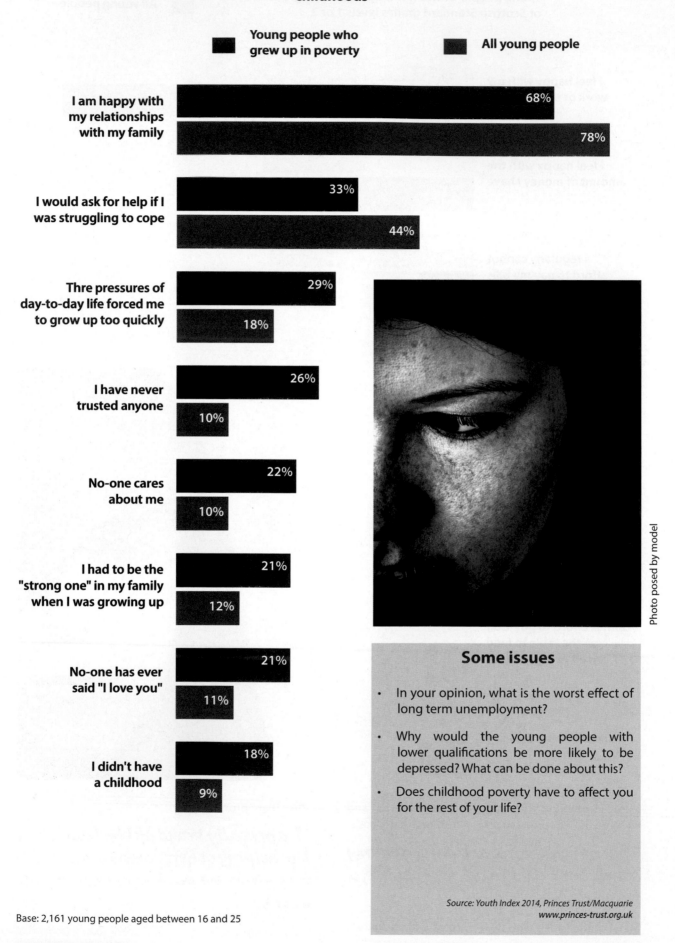

I am happy with my relationships with my family
- 68%
- 78%

I would ask for help if I was struggling to cope
- 33%
- 44%

Thre pressures of day-to-day life forced me to grow up too quickly
- 29%
- 18%

I have never trusted anyone
- 26%
- 10%

No-one cares about me
- 22%
- 10%

I had to be the "strong one" in my family when I was growing up
- 21%
- 12%

No-one has ever said "I love you"
- 21%
- 11%

I didn't have a childhood
- 18%
- 9%

Photo posed by model

Base: 2,161 young people aged between 16 and 25

Some issues

- In your opinion, what is the worst effect of long term unemployment?

- Why would the young people with lower qualifications be more likely to be depressed? What can be done about this?

- Does childhood poverty have to affect you for the rest of your life?

Source: Youth Index 2014, Princes Trust/Macquarie
www.princes-trust.org.uk

What bothers young people?

Young people are having to deal with serious issues... and they are facing these concerns at a younger age

In 2012/13 ChildLine counselled **147,302 girls**, **48,351 boys** and **83,233 where gender was not given**

Top five reasons young people contacted ChildLine, by gender

- ■ **Number of girls**
- ■ **Number of boys**
- ■ **Gender of the young person was not known**

Depression/unhappiness eg feeling sad, low mood, lonely, low self-esteem or body image issues

- 19,054
- 5,208
- 11,679

Family relationships eg conflict/arguments, parents' divorce/separation

- 18,537
- 5,556
- 11,061

Bullying/cyberbullying eg peer-to-peer bullying

- 14,653
- 6,724
- 9,010

> Self-harm was up **41%** from 2011/12.
> Girls were 15 times more likely than boys to contact ChildLine with this concern.
>
> Contact about suicidal thoughts/ feelings rose **33%** from 2011/12.

Self-harm eg intentional self-injury

- 12,643
- 856
- 9,033

Suicidal issues eg actively suicidal or thoughts/feelings of suicide

- 8,461
- 1,579
- 4,823

Children and young people don't have to tell ChildLine their age, but age was revealed in 63% of counselling sessions.

Top 5 concerns, by age group

11 and under

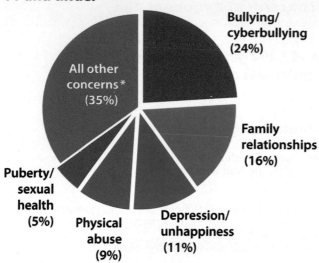

All other concerns* (35%)

Bullying/ cyberbullying (24%)

Family relationships (16%)

Depression/ unhappiness (11%)

Physical abuse (9%)

Puberty/ sexual health (5%)

13% of counselling sessions - **22,733** children - were within this age group. **86%** of these callers were aged between 9-11.

The youngest recorded age was five.

*eg sexual abuse and online sexual abuse, physical health & illness, school or education problems, problems with friends, loss and bereavement

12 to 15 year olds

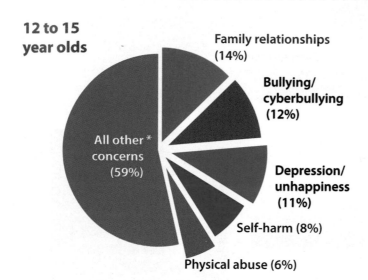

All other * concerns (59%)

Family relationships (14%)

Bullying/ cyberbullying (12%)

Depression/ unhappiness (11%)

Self-harm (8%)

Physical abuse (6%)

56% of counselling was with this age group - **97,685** counselling sessions.

The majority of counselling was with 12-15 year olds and most callers were aged 15.

*eg sexual abuse and online sexual abuse, problems with friends, puberty & sexual health, suicidal issues, school or education problem

16 to 18 year olds

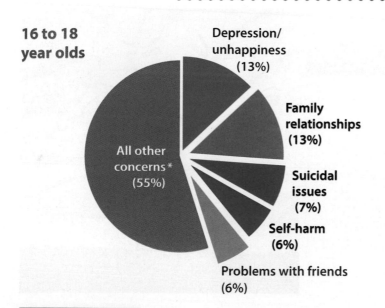

All other concerns* (55%)

Depression/ unhappiness (13%)

Family relationships (13%)

Suicidal issues (7%)

Self-harm (6%)

Problems with friends (6%)

31% of counselling was with 16-18 year olds - **54,003** young people.

*eg sexual abuse and online sexual abuse, mental health issues, puberty & sexual health, pregnancy & parenting, bullying/online bullying

How young people contacted ChildLine

The number of online counselling sessions increased by **13%** from 2011/12. This meant that, for the first time ever, more children and young people were counselled online eg by either 1-2-1 chats or email – than by phone.

Of those who got in touch about self-harm, suicide and mental health issues, **78%** chose to do so online instead of on the phone.

58% of counselling took place over the phone when young people needed help with issues relating to abuse.

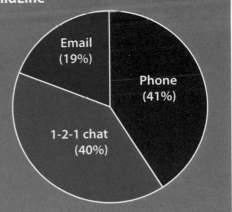

Email (19%)
Phone (41%)
1-2-1 chat (40%)

Taboo

Self-harm, suicidal issues and mental health concerns are often viewed as taboo subjects by young people and therefore they might find it harder to talk about their feelings on these subjects.

Contacting ChildLine online rather than by phone creates a 'safe' distance for the young person to share their feelings and explore the issues they're experiencing.

**ChildLine:
0800 1111**

Some issues

- Why are the numbers for girls so much higher than for boys?

- Why do you think so many young people didn't state their gender?

- Are there any reasons for the different concerns of different age groups?

- How useful are organisations like ChildLine?

See also Self-harm, p186

Source: Can I tell you something? ChildLine Review 2012/13
www.childline.org.uk

Self-harm

Self-harm seems to be increasing as young people deal with stress

What is self-harm?

It describes a range of deliberate actions that people do to themselves. It can involve:

- cutting;
- burning;
- scalding;
- banging or scratching one's own body;
- breaking bones;
- hair pulling;
- swallowing poisonous substances or objects

Photo posed by model

Why do people self-harm?

One of the most common myths is that self-harm is about 'attention seeking'. In fact, most self-harm is actually done in secret, for a long time and it can be very hard for young people to find enough courage to ask for help.

Many people self-harm to 'get out the hurt, anger and pain' caused by pressures in their lives when they don't know what else to do or don't feel they have any other options.

For some young people, self-harm gives temporary relief and a sense of control over their lives but brings its own, very serious, problems.

"I am getting bullied at school. They are saying really nasty things and telling me it would be better if I wasn't here. I have been self-harming because I need a release... I don't want the scars, but I need to cut and I need to suffer"

Girl aged 14

Reasons why young people may self-harm

- Being bullied at school;
- Family problems eg not getting on with parents, other family members, divorce;
- Stress and worry about school work and exams;
- Feeling isolated;

- Bereavement;
- Unwanted pregnancy;
- Abuse (in childhood or current) physical, sexual or verbal;
- The self-harm or suicide of someone close to them;

- Problems to do with sexuality, race, culture or religion;
- Low self-esteem;
- Feelings of rejection socially or within their families

How many young people self-harm?

In 2012/13 ChildLine counselled **22,532** young people whose main concern was self-harm - **8%** of all the counselling that took place that year.

There was a total of almost **47,000** counselling sessions in which self harm was mentioned - a **41%** increase on the previous year.

Almost **33%** of those young people told ChildLine that they had very recently self-harmed. **42%** said they had been self-harming for years and that it was ongoing.

Age

70% of the contact ChildLine received about self-harm came from young people aged between 12-15.

In 2011/12 self-harm was a top five concern for 14 year olds. In 2012/13, it featured as a top five concern for 13 year olds for the first time.

There was nearly a **50%** rise in contacts with 12 year olds about self-harm – the highest increase of any age.

NB These figures only include cases where the age of the young person was known.

Self-harm and feeling suicidal

Young people who self-harm hurt themselves as a way of coping with life, not necessarily with a view to ending it.

During 2012/13, **34%** of the young people who contacted ChildLine about suicidal feelings, also mentioned self-harm.

So for some young people, there is a link between using self-harm to block out their mental anguish and feeling so overwhelmed that they consider or attempt to end their own lives.

"I have been self-harming for a few years now... I do it so I can deal with the pain of what he does to me. I haven't told anyone about what's happening not even my family. I want to stop hurting myself but I can't stop myself. I am in a routine of doing it now and when the pain of everything gets too much it helps to take it away"

Girl aged 16

Gender divide

Girls self-harming outnumber boys by 15:1.

There was a **37%** increase in self-harm counselling with girls in 2012/13, compared with just **10%** with boys.

Photo posed by model

What if you need help?

If you are self-harming, talk to someone you feel comfortable speaking to. This could be your mum or dad, a teacher, a doctor, or an adult that you feel you can trust.

You might like to speak to a helpline first and practise the conversation with them, to help build your confidence.

You might also find it helpful to keep a diary, or to write a letter to the person, which you could share with them when you are ready.

Photo posed by model

How you can help someone

ChildLine received over **1,500** contacts from young people who were concerned about someone who was self-harming.

If you are worried about someone:

- make time to gently and sympathetically discuss the problem with them and listen to what they say without judging them or being critical

- try to appreciate how difficult they are finding life and show them you understand

- discuss the possibility of seeking professional help

- get medical help if any injuries are serious

- it's important not to react in a strongly negative or critical way (such as getting angry), as this kind of reaction is likely to make the problem worse

- if they don't want to discuss their self-harm with you, perhaps suggest they speak to an anonymous helpline or see their GP

Friends and family can also get advice from the organisations below.

I hurt myself today. I kept smashing my head against the wall because I felt so angry with everything. I don't feel like anyone cares about me... I think I might need some help

Boy aged 15

Useful organisations

ChildLine: 0800 1111
www.childline.org.uk
Samaritans: 08457 90 90 90
YoungMinds: 020 7089 5050
Parent Helpline: 0808 802 5544
www.youngminds.org.uk
Harmless:
www.harmless.org.uk
National Self Harm Network:
0800 622 6000
Lifesigns:
www.lifesigns.org.uk

Some issues

- Can you understand why someone would say "I need to suffer"?

- Why do you think that the numbers of younger people who self-harm are going up?

- What action should people take if they find that someone is self-harming?

- Is this just something people grow out of?

Source: The truth about self-harm, Mental Health Foundation
www.mentalhealth.org.uk
Can I tell you something? ChildLine Review 2012/13
www.childline.org.uk
NHS Choices www.nhs.uk

Looking forward

The views of young people growing up in uncertain times

Greatest ambitions in life
(Top five answers)

To have a happy family life	64%
To have a job that you enjoy	54%
Being successful in your career	38%
To make your parents proud	28%
To travel the world	27%

To be *famous - 1%* and to be *rich - 5%* were their lowest priorities

"There are a lot of expectations on young people today to earn lots of money and to wear the latest trends. But I'd rather be happy than rich."

Jonathan, 18

Inspiration in life
(Top five answers)

Mother	61%
Friends	55%
Father	54%
Teachers	45%
Grandparents	36%

Photo posed by models

Despite growing up in a celebrity-obsessed culture, young people are more likely to be Inspired by family and friends than celebrities - just *21%* said that a celebrity was a role model

"I most admire people like my mum who always goes out of her way to help other people, than celebrities who have too much money and have lost touch with reality..."

Hannah, 17

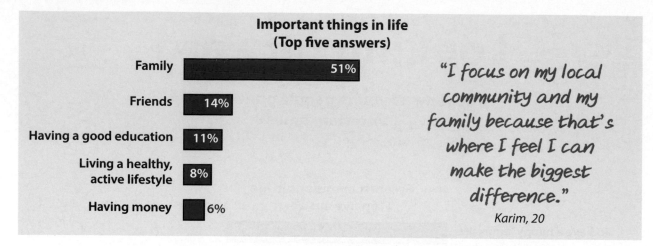

Important things in life
(Top five answers)

Family	51%
Friends	14%
Having a good education	11%
Living a healthy, active lifestyle	8%
Having money	6%

"I focus on my local community and my family because that's where I feel I can make the biggest difference."

Karim, 20

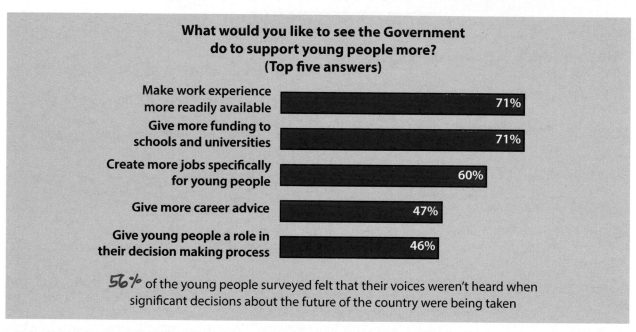

What would you like to see the Government do to support young people more?
(Top five answers)

Make work experience more readily available	71%
Give more funding to schools and universities	71%
Create more jobs specifically for young people	60%
Give more career advice	47%
Give young people a role in their decision making process	46%

56% of the young people surveyed felt that their voices weren't heard when significant decisions about the future of the country were being taken

"I'm studying politics because I want to make a difference to the world...
...it's up to us to try to change things for the better."

Jayden 18

Photo posed by models

Media portrayal

Young People thought that soaps and reality TV shows portrayed young people as irresponsible and anti-social and felt that this influenced how other generations feel about them.

- **83%** thought the media portrayed young people based on stereotypes rather than reality;

- **77%** thought the media made people more hostile towards young people;

- **74%** thought positive things that young people do went unnoticed by the media;

- **72%** thought the media made people afraid of young people;

- Only **12%** thought the media represented young people fairly.

"When I am out with my friends, I can see elderly people being nervous and scared at seeing a group of young people - it makes me sick to think that I am making someone feel like that."

Vicky, 21

Worries

Many reported having worries about the impact of economic recession:

- **72%** of young people were worried about being able to afford to buy a home;

- **66%** were worried about finding a job.

- **56%** said the economic recession made them less optimistic about the future.

Optimism

- **83%** said it was the little things in life that made them happy;

- **80%** were excited about their future;

- **77%** were optimistic about what the following year would bring;

- **65%** thought that good far outweighed the bad in life.

"Young people have had to change their expectations a lot - suddenly moving out and having my own home just isn't realistic... it's definitely tough out there for us."

Alex 22

Some issues

- What stereotypes of young people are used by the media?

- Do you agree with these views about the future and what is important?

- How could you persuade the government and other decision makers to listen to young people?

Base: 1,023 16-24 year olds and a series of specialist youth focus groups

Source: Populus survey for Coca-Cola Great Britain
www.coca-cola.co.uk

Index

Entries in **colour** refer to main sections. Page numbers refer to the first page. Most charts contain UK or GB information.

A

Abortion 112
Accent 122
Afghanistan 154, 156, 164
ANIMALS 7-14
ART & CULTURE 15-24 & 36

B

Blogs 16, 160
BODY IMAGE 25-34 & 54, 99
BRITAIN & ITS CITIZENS 35-48 & 70, 125, 128, 150, 154
BULLYING 49-60 & 183

C

Celebrity 39, 178
Charity 150, 168
ChildLine 52, 86, 186
Children see **BULLYING, YOUNG PEOPLE** & 26, 62, 64, 66, 68, 80, 84, 86, 99, 134, 136, 142
China 160, 166
Climate change see **ENVIRONMENT**
Consumers 76, 92, 94, 96, 138
Cosmetic surgery 30
Crime see **LAW & ORDER**
Culture see **ART & CULTURE**
Cyberbullying see **BULLYING** & 131
Cycling 144

D

Death 115, 118, 154, 156, 162, 166, 172, 174
Debt 89, 92
Developing world see **WIDER WORLD**
Diet 26, 118
Disasters 166
Divorce 86

E

Earthquake 162, 166
Ebola 172
EDUCATION 61-70 & 89, 180, 189
Employment see Work
ENVIRONMENT 71-78
Equality see **GENDER** & 26, 28, 144
Ethnicity 52, 134

F

Facebook 58
FAMILY & RELATIONSHIPS 79-87 & 94, 102, 180,183, 189
FINANCE 88-97 & 64, 76, 82, 138, 144, 150, 168, 174, 189
Football 144,148
Fraud 138
Free speech 104, 156, 158, 160

G

GENDER 98-105 & 26, 28, 30, 82, 134, 144
Girlguiding 26, 80, 99
Graffiti 18
Greenhouse gases see **ENVIRONMENT**

H

HEALTH 106-120 & 72, 172, 174
Holidays 125, 128
Housing 82, 189
Human rights 104, 156, 158, 160

I

Iceland 164
India 166, 168
Inequality see equality
Inflation 96
Internet see **BULLYING** & 16, 66, 156, 160
Iran 160
Iraq 156
ISIS 156

J

Johansson, Scarlett 39
Journalists 156, 158, 160

L

LANGUAGE 121-129 & 36
LAW & ORDER 130-140 & 112
Leisure 16, 20, 22, 24, 125, 128
Lone parents 82

M

Malaria 174
Manners 36, 44, 46
Marriage 84, 86
Media 16, 26, 144, 156, 158, 160, 189
Mental health 180, 183, 186
Money see **FINANCE**
Museums 16, 20, 24

N

Neighbours 44

O

Olympics 144

P

Parents see **FAMILY & RELATIONSHIPS** & 39, 66, 89, 102, 142, 183, 189
Peace 162, 164
Pets 11, 14
Phobia 48
Plastic surgery 30
Police 134
Politics 42
Pollution see **ENVIRONMENT**
Poverty 64, 180
Pregnancy 112
Prison 160

R

Race 52, 134
Rape 131
Reading 16, 22
Religion 68, 84
Role models 39, 178, 189
Royalty 39

S

Salt 118
School 52, 62-68, 136, 142
Science 8
Self-harm 54, 183, 186
Sexism see equality
Sexual issues 84, 131, 183
Shopping see Consumers
Social media see **BULLYING** & 156, 160
SPORT 141-152 & 178
Students 70, 89
Suicide 54, 183
Syria 164

T

Tattoos 32
Theft 136, 138
Tourism 125, 128
Traffic 74
Transport 74, 76
Turkey 160
TV 16, 144
Twitter 58

U

United Nations 162
University 70, 89

V

Violence see **BULLYING, WAR & CONFLICT** & 131, 136, 183
Volunteering 168

W

WAR & CONFLICT 153-164
Weather 36, 166
WIDER WORLD 165-176, see also **WAR & CONFLICT** & 148
Women see **GENDER** & 26, 28, 30, 112, 131, 144, 178
Work 80, 110, 122, 156, 158, 180, 189
World Cup 144, 148

Y

YOUNG PEOPLE 177-191, see also **BULLYING, EDUCATION, FAMILY & RELATIONSHIPS** & 26, 42, 89, 99, 115, 134, 136, 142